THE INTANGIBLE
YOU
UNMASKING
YOUR UNIQUENESS

Copyright © 2023 by Flowcess®

No part of this book may be reproduced in any form or by any means—electronic, mechanical, photocopying, recording, or otherwise—without written permission of the publisher or author. The exception would be in the case of brief quotations embodied in the critical articles or reviews and pages where permission is specifically granted by the publisher or author. For permission requests, please contact Flowcess at info@flowcess.com.

Cover art design and illustrations by Alaina Albaugh
Book design by Mark D'Antoni, eBook DesignWorks

ISBN: 979-8-9856838-1-3

flowcess.com

CONTENTS

Foreword	5
Introduction	11
CHAPTER 1 **Car and Driver**	21
CHAPTER 2 **Intangible Drivers®**	30
CHAPTER 3 **Perceiver**	41
CHAPTER 4 **Teacher**	60
CHAPTER 5 **Compassion**	77
CHAPTER 6 **Giver**	95
CHAPTER 7 **Server**	111
CHAPTER 8 **Administrator**	131
CHAPTER 9 **Exhorter**	152
CHAPTER 10 **Determining The Uniqueness Of Others**	174
CHAPTER 11 **Healthy Relationships**	182
CHAPTER 12 **Trauma, Dysfunction, And Unhealthy Relationships**	193
CHAPTER 13 **Generativity**	201

"Knowing yourself is the beginning of all wisdom."

—Aristotle

FOREWORD

By Dr. Ellie Harper

IN OCTOBER 2020, I met an irrepressible Scotsman called Colin Stevenson. On paper, our lives look very different, but on a deeper level, I knew we were two of a kind, and we clicked right away. He had so much energy it was catching! "What's his secret?" I wondered.

We soon got to talking about what we both did for a living. I told him I was a psychologist. His eyes lit up. "There's a reason you and I met," he said with a smile. "What would you say if I told you that I could share information with you that would not only transform your life but also mean that you could help thousands of people?"

I looked at him intently. Something told me he was genuine. "I'd say: Surely, that's what it's all about."

The next time we spoke, Colin took me through the Intangible Driver quiz on the Flowcess website. I came out Compassion-Server. He told me a little about what that meant and signposted me to two videos on his YouTube channel, *Health, Happiness and Flow*, which explained it in more detail.

As I watched the Compassion Why video, I was gobsmacked. They were literally describing me! Yes, I can instantly tell who is in the most pain when I walk into a room. Yes, I get upset when other people say I'm too emotional. Yes, 99% of the time, I'm one of the nicest people you'll ever meet, but every now and then, it all gets too much, and I hulk out!

No wonder I'm the person at a party new acquaintances will end up pouring their hearts out to. No wonder I have a reputation as "The Peacemaker" among friends and family and am often called upon to help settle disputes. No wonder I had been drawn to the field of psychology and ended up working in a role with people with complex and enduring mental health problems. These were the people in the most pain. I had a natural ability to bear that pain. It's WHO I AM.

I moved on to the Server How video. More incredulity! Yes, I spring into action when I see an unfilled need. Yes, I feel drained when you tell me I HAVE to do something. Yes, I have a hard time saying no to people.

As soon as they started talking about the ability of Server Hows to move between the Intangible Drivers to meet people's needs, I was instantly transported back to my school days, where three years in a row at the annual prize-giving ceremony, I won the award for "Best All-Rounder".

No wonder that in all the various jobs I had done before settling on a career as a psychologist, I always did well. You can put me in pretty much any situation and, as long as there are needs to be met, I'll figure out how to adapt and thrive.

After watching the videos, my head was buzzing with questions and thoughts about all the potential implications of understanding my own and other people's Intangible Drivers. This explained so much! I had to know more.

Colin introduced me to John Lenhart at Flowcess, and I took their Instant Impact course. I quickly set about figuring out the Intangible Drivers of my family and friends.

The impact of learning this information on my personal life was immediate and profound. In a short space of time, my mental health, relationships and self-esteem all improved. Daily interactions became easier because I knew how to embrace my own uniqueness and connect with the Intangible Drivers of others.

Perhaps most importantly, it meant I could bond with my young daughter on a whole new level. She's a Perceiver-Server, always wanting to make others aware by filling needs. I suddenly realised that her superpower is that she sees a world of opportunity, and she wants to share that with the rest of us!

Now, rather than get frustrated with the countless exclamations of "Look, Mummy!" I receive over the day, I have a newfound appreciation for her hawk-eye abilities and can connect with her instantly simply by responding, "I see that!"

Over the next few months, I learnt more about the Intangible Drivers and the Flowcess model for the mind and brain. After experiencing the life-changing impact of understanding the Intangible Drivers for myself, my mind quickly turned to how I could apply this in my work with my clients and to the field of psychology more broadly.

> MY MIND QUICKLY TURNED TO HOW I COULD APPLY THIS IN MY WORK WITH MY CLIENTS.

I got into psychology out of a genuine desire to help people. I gain so much energy when people share their pain with me, and I'm able to help them heal and grow. It turns out that's what Compassion-Servers are made for! Seeing my clients get better just gives me the best feeling in the world!

And yet, throughout my career, I had developed a growing sense of unease. Several things were bothering me. I couldn't get my head around why therapy seemed to work for some clients and not others. Or why sessions with some clients seemed to flow effortlessly, while with others, every session felt like an uphill struggle.

I was increasingly disturbed by the number of clients who came in and out of therapy without gaining meaningful or lasting benefits. Worst of all, I could see that sometimes, therapy was making people WORSE!

A deep-rooted sense of restlessness and frustration had taken hold of me and wouldn't budge, no matter how hard I tried to muscle through and crack on with the job. Helping some of the people some of the time wasn't enough.

When people come into therapy, they're in a hole. Psychological therapy, in its various guises, can help people get out of a hole. That's good, right? I wasn't so sure. Because then what? How do you stay out of a hole and get up the mountain to a life of ongoing growth and fulfilment?

Even after a "successful" course of therapy, clients were only ever one traumatic life event away from falling back into a hole. And sometimes they were so freaked out when they got out of the hole that they jumped right back in! I saw it all the time. For some people, being a person who is "mentally ill" had become so ingrained in how they saw themselves that being "well" was just too much of a daunting prospect. When you don't know who you truly are, the hole feels like a safe place.

I realised we weren't giving people the help they REALLY needed, the help that would mean that they could move forward in their lives, gaining energy and happiness without the risk of ending up back in a hole. Why not? Because as it stands, psychology doesn't have the means. We are limited by the boundaries of our current understanding of the human mind and brain.

Learning the Flowcess information was a huge lightbulb moment for me and a pivotal turning point in my career. I suddenly understood a person's Intangible Drivers, their uniqueness, who they are at the level of their mind and soul is what psychology is missing.

Getting a person up the mountain means growing their self-esteem. It means helping them to understand, embrace and take ownership of their uniqueness. When you can do that, every situation, every circumstance, every interaction becomes an opportunity to bring out more of your uniqueness and to GAIN energy. That's how you stay out of a hole. That's how you get up the mountain. That's where THE REAL HELP HAPPENS.

This is by no means an attack on the psychology profession. I have worked in the field for over a decade and had the privilege of meeting many intelligent, talented and caring souls who are genuinely doing the best they can to help their clients with the tools they've got.

> LEARNING THE FLOWCESS INFORMATION WAS A HUGE LIGHTBULB MOMENT FOR ME.

Instead, this is a call to action to those among my friends and colleagues who are ready to embrace a growth mindset and progress psychology to where it ought to be: at the forefront of understanding the human mind and brain so we can dissolve human suffering and facilitate human growth.

I know I am by no means alone in my desire to help more people in more meaningful ways. I see how psychologists across the field are embracing eclecticism, pluralism and integrative approaches — all reflections of our collective endeavours to deliver more effective and meaningful interventions tailored to each unique individual.

But there is a simpler way. I am now applying my knowledge of the Intangible Drivers in my work with clients daily. Knowing the Intangible Drivers of my clients makes my job easier and more fun. It also means that I can help people from the first session intentionally and help them up the mountain once they're out of the hole!

The feedback I'm getting from my clients is incredible. I see the same profound impact in their lives that I experienced in mine. Clients who came to me at the end of their tether, many of whom have been in the mental health system for years without making any significant progress, are transforming their lives.

I'm still doing what I did before, but now I'm supplementing my work with the powerful information in this book, and my first step is ALWAYS to figure out the uniqueness of the individual. That way, I can tailor my approach to who they are from the outset and give them the tools they need to understand themselves and live their best lives.

Going forward, I believe that the Intangible Drivers have to be part of psychology. It's the difference between hoping for the best and helping people on purpose. It's the greater system that can make sense of human behaviour. It's the TRUTH from which all the principles and applications within psychology stem.

Step one of human psychology IS understanding a person's uniqueness. We just didn't know it. Until now.

—Dr. Ellie Harper
Human Flow Psychologist

INTRODUCTION

NOTHING CURES a lonely heart like sex, drugs, and rock 'n' roll!

My name is Jonathan, and that was my plan for happiness. What's yours?

I want you to think of your favorite song. How do you feel when you hear it? Does it make you feel alive? Do you want to sing it, or dance to it, or share it with others? I want you to feel that same exhilaration about your life. In fact, I want your life to BE your favorite song. The kind of life where you wake up every day excited to live it and share it with others.

You and I are unique. There is a version of ourselves, beneath all the hopes and dreams, beneath all the education and jobs, beneath all the friends and family, that is fundamentally who we are at our core. We can feel it. Who are you?

You are not the "you" that you pretend to be at parties in hopes that other people find you interesting. Not the idealized "you" that appears in all your social media feeds. Not the professional or corporate "you" whom you become at work in order to stay employed and climb the career ladder. Not the "you" that you present to potential romantic partners when you're flirting in those first few exhilarating encounters, hoping to impress them.

I want you to understand the real YOU. The YOU who you feel safe being in front of your most trusted friends and loved ones. The weird, odd, quirky YOU that maybe no one else gets to see. The YOU that sings off-key in the shower, who dances around the house like a dork when you play your favorite song.

When was the last time someone has expressed a desire to know more of that YOU? Have they ever? How would you feel to know that someone wants to deeply understand the real you?

Why would others want to understand you? Because you are unique! There is no one else on this planet exactly like you! That makes you valuable. Therefore, knowing *you* will bring others a type of value they couldn't experience without you.

When you know who you are uniquely, you'll know how to live and thrive in the value that is uniquely yours, and you are then free to give that value to the world! This is the key to unassailable psychological strength, boundless energy, and vibrant health. That's what this book is all about - unmasking the real you so you can have the happiness and joy that should have always been yours.

Part of that mask that we hide behind is a plan for happiness that doesn't work, and mine was my music career. I was a member of a band traveling throughout North America, surrounded by fans, drugs, women, and just enough money to continue the journey. We were chasing the next deal, recording in Los Angeles with sought-after producers, and touring non-stop.

I made it! A dream come true! And as soon as I made it, I began a downward spiral into despair. The longer the band continued, the more unhappy and alone I felt. That feeling of being alone came from a deep wound that I had been carrying around since I was a kid.

When I was eleven, my family moved from Canada to the United States and settled in a small town in Wisconsin. I enrolled at a new school and was excited to meet new friends. I can remember that first day so clearly. I was teased by teachers and fellow students because I was from Canada. I tried to laugh along. I held out hope for meeting friends as I entered the lunchroom, but I quickly realized I didn't know anyone, and no one welcomed me. I ended up sitting at a table all by myself to eat my lunch.

After a rough start, I eventually made friends at the new school, but I never forgot the pain of feeling alone. I hated the feeling of being disconnected, and it motivated me to do whatever I could to be a part of a group. I played sports. I sang in musicals. I even won the "nicest student award" in the first year I moved. I discovered that not only was I athletic, but I could also play the drums. In high school, I met some guys who wanted me to join their band. I didn't know it at the time, but I was convinced that this was the answer to never feeling lonely again. I was willing to do anything to keep that band going. The group that I would grow old with was here!

For as long as I can remember, I have had a sense of destiny. I have always desired to be part of something impactful, deeply connected with friends so that we would change the world together. Playing in the band was how I felt that could be accomplished. We played together for eight years, steadily increasing our skill and reputation until we were touring the country with some of the biggest acts of the day.

But, the bigger we got, the more unsettled I began to feel. I didn't see the band changing the world, and I was feeling more disconnected from my purpose. I began to feel that little eleven-year-old creeping up on me with tears pouring down his face to remind me that I was still there, alone and afraid. I tried to drown him out with music, busyness, parties, and women. It didn't work.

Our band was performing at the Winter X-Games when that little boy finally caught me. I was staying at a beautiful lodge in the mountains of Colorado with my bandmates. One of the perks of playing in Aspen, Colorado was that we got to ski in The Rockies. I stood on that mountain top, looking down at how far my dream had taken me, and I felt more alone than ever. The eleven-year-old boy at the lunch table now had his opportunity to get a stranglehold on me. He was forcing me to look at my life and realize I still felt like an eleven-year-old alone at the lunch table.

I didn't believe our music was doing anything to change the world. The only thing I was using it for was to serve myself by not feeling alone. The drugs, the shows, the parties, and the women made me experience highs and lows that led to nowhere. In the quiet times of early mornings, I would often wonder how I would feel if my sister threw herself at a man she didn't know. It made me feel worse. I was lost.

It was gut-wrenching to have to wonder if attaining my dream didn't lead to happiness, then was it even possible to be happy? How could I have been so wrong? Was I to spend the rest of my years dragging myself from one moment to the next in an effort just to survive? Was there no purpose for my life?

I decided to pack my bags and move back in with my parents. I struggled mentally and emotionally, trying to think about where I went wrong and what my purpose was. I am grateful for my parents because they gave me a safe place to struggle and pick up the pieces of my broken life.

One day a friend told me that there was an answer, that I did have a purpose, and it was possible for me to understand my purpose and to achieve it intentionally. And the best news was that living out my purpose would not end with me being sad and alone at the top of a mountain. It would be the source of my energy and lead to healthy happiness and joy. The answer was beyond playing music. In fact, he likened who I am to being an instrument. He told me, "If you unlock who you are, your instrument, then you can LIVE music!"

He and a few of his friends came down to visit me, and I marveled at the way these people spoke to each other. It was like a different language. With it, they had this secret key to unlock depths of understanding about one another that brought them closer than any band I had ever experienced. It was as if they knew themselves like a virtuoso musician knows their own instrument. There was a respect and admiration for what made them all different. They saw the value in the other person playing a different "instrument" than them, and there was life in the room.

Being with them made me feel like I was being pulled up into a higher state of self-awareness, of connection, of music. I felt like I was being taken to a place beyond myself, a place that was different, uncomfortable, and really exciting. It felt like a place I was always meant to be, and I wanted more. They befriended me and began to teach me what they had learned. I began to unlock my instrument.

> **THE GOOD NEWS IS THAT HAPPINESS IS NOT OUT OF REACH. IT'S POSSIBLE. IT'S YOURS FOR THE TAKING!**

This was my first step on a journey that has changed my life. As I now travel and meet with others who are seeking their healthy happiness, the stories are so similar. There is a shared passion for discovering and living out who we were created to be, but understanding who we were created to be often seems to be out of reach.

The good news is that happiness is not out of reach. It's possible. It's yours for the taking! And the key to that vibrant state of happiness is living and thriving in your uniqueness. You already know this, but you've never been able to put words to it. This book will give you those words.

Best of all, when you truly and deeply understand the real you, you can help others understand you as well. You can show them how to communicate with you in ways that will give you energy and motivation. And you can finally be genuinely and deeply understood by others. You can be known, accepted, cherished, and even loved on a deeper level than you ever thought possible.

You can be the YOU whom you wish EVERYONE knew.

I meant what I said earlier about this book unmasking the real you because every other attempt you've made to understand the real you and what motivates and energizes you only focuses on the mask that you put on every day.

When I first encountered the technology in this book, I was skeptical. Was this just another personality test?

The famed Myers-Briggs evaluation told me that I was an INTP (Introvert, Intuitive, Thinking, Perceptive). I was called an introvert because I tend to shut down in situations where I have to interact with many people at once, but I never really considered myself shy. In fact, when I'm in a comfortable situation, you can't shut me up! I love talking about topics I'm passionate about and learning the stories of others. Moreover, I'm an excellent public speaker. I get energized sharing my story with large groups of people to help them understand their value. How could they say I was an introvert but also be someone who loves sharing in front of thousands of people?

So what did I do? I took other types of personality tests to see if there was a trend. I took DiSC, Enneagram, Strengthsfinder, Love Languages, astrology, etc.

The limitation is that those personality tests can only describe the mask you put on when you're under stress and want to portray a particular person to the rest of the world. But they are unable to identify who you are at your core. At best, a personality test can predict how you may behave in certain circumstances. But you are not your behavior! You are so much more than that.

Knowing your uniqueness is the key to finding healthy relationships, improving the relationships you are in currently, selecting the ideal job, getting along with family members, parenting your children, overcoming addiction, disarming abusers, and ensuring that you are not inadvertently being a bully yourself.

When you know who you are intangibly, you are in control. You are no longer subject to the whims of others. You can be resilient and thrive in any situation, and intentionally get energy regardless of the circumstance.

For a long time, I didn't want to accept that reality. I replaced identifying who I am with my passion for music, treating that passion like it was my identity. It required me to put on a mask and live and act in accordance with that role.

I've noticed that most people follow the same path and miss the opportunity to embrace their uniqueness. They claim that doing things and having things are who they are: their physical characteristics, their profession, their hobby, their money or material possessions, or their roles such as a wife or parent *is* their identity. *I'm a doctor. I'm a dad. I'm wealthy. I'm an American. I'm an athlete. I'm a homeowner. I'm a brunette. I'm bald.*

That tends to be as deep as most people can pursue because that is how far the field of psychology has matured in identifying the single most important thing that can help people with their happiness, which is discovering your uniqueness.

Worst of all, if you don't know your uniqueness, you may begin to identify with the behavior you display when you are in dysfunction or a bad spot mentally and emotionally. You'll start to think of yourself as shy, awkward, a pessimist, short-tempered, indecisive, an alcoholic, obsessive-compulsive, needy, manipulative, etc. Tragically, in our search for self, we often let our behaviors define us.

Again, I was one of those people who loved taking a personality test. I felt it could lead me to understand myself more. Over time, I realized my profile was changing. The tests would tell me that was normal. That we change over time. We're evolving.

But that made me feel very disappointed because it seemed like I was constantly trying to catch up in understanding who I am versus completely understanding who I am so that I can intentionally drive my life. As my personality test results shifted over time, I felt further away from understanding the real me. And I was meeting many people who felt the same way.

Because the circumstances of our lives don't stay static but are constantly changing, we evolve and grow as individuals in response. Millions of stimuli come at us every day, and each night our brain processes all those stimuli, resulting in a changed brain each and every day. There are no zero events to the brain, meaning every stimulus affects our brain and changes it. So, our behaviors also change over time. *That* is what personality tests measure.

If I work in a job that requires me to be conscientious and then get promoted to a position that requires me to drive for results, a personality test will show that shift in my behaviors.

What it doesn't tell me is who I am at my core — the real *me* that doesn't change. We need a trait that can define our *uniqueness*, our intrinsic motivation. That fundamental aspect of who we are that underlies everything we do for our entire lives, regardless of our circumstances. I needed to know what made me, *me*.

I found that answer, and it has changed my entire life. I know who I am, and I discovered my purpose. I was blessed to find a wife that was the perfect fit for the real me, and her purpose is aligned with mine. I end each year with more energy and passion than I did the previous year. I am truly living my best life. And you can too!

That's the journey I am offering you with this book. I want to take you on the same journey of self-discovery that I went on without all the bumps and hassles that I did.

We are fortunate to live in a time where neuroscience has proven out theories that take us past the behavior science of psychology. We can understand the wiring in our brain and how that affects our thinking and responses.

This book will focus on the first step in that process, the Intangible Driver. This is who you are at your core. The real YOU. Your instrument. It is intangible, meaning you can't see it, but it drives everything you do.

Your Intangible Driver, or ID, will allow you to define the first part of your actual uniqueness, and for the first time in your life, you'll have words that can describe how you've experienced your entire life. Words that have been true since your childhood and will stay true until your last breath.

Learning my Intangible Driver was the first time I felt like I had the information to understand myself truly. To fully understand who I was as that little boy, alone in the lunchroom, to the young adult seeking affirmation and happiness from the world, to the man I am today.

Not only have I been through the journey to discover my own uniqueness that resulted in energy, passion, and fulfillment, but I have been fortunate to coach executives, managers, pastors, and teachers and watch them reach the same discoveries. And the best part is it's not a fad. It's not information that is fun and trendy to dabble in but then forgotten. I use the understanding that I have of my ID more over time.

I cannot tell you all the testimonies I receive, years after helping someone, where this information continues to help them improve their lives and the lives of those they care about, more and more with each passing year.

They share that they have been able to intentionally date, get married, have children, embrace friendships, and flourish in their occupations, all because they took time to understand their Intangible Driver and how to determine the ID of others.

I've always been filled with a passion for changing the world, and I knew if I could get the proper understanding, I could work tirelessly to help people find healthy happiness.

> **WORDS THAT HAVE BEEN TRUE SINCE YOUR CHILDHOOD AND WILL STAY TRUE UNTIL YOUR LAST BREATH.**

At the end of the day, I liken all of us to instruments. Who we are, our uniqueness, is an instrument that only we are qualified to play, but it's limited in how impactful it can be alone. When we learn how to play that instrument with others, we become part of a band.

This is my life's purpose: to help others live a life of music. If you want your life to be your favorite song but need a guide to bring it out, you are in the right recording studio... I mean place.

Are you ready to discover your Intangible Driver?

CHAPTER 1

CAR AND DRIVER

IF A CAR goes off the road, is it a good thing or a bad thing?

The obvious answer is that it's a bad thing, right? But what are the reasons a car might go off the road? It might be an internal issue such as a faulty brake line that causes the vehicle to go off the road. Or an external circumstance, such as hitting a patch of ice while going around a corner at forty-five miles an hour.

The behavior of other drivers can also send us off the road. If I'm driving down the highway and a Mack truck is coming straight at me in the wrong lane, it's actually a good move for me to go off the road to get out of the way!

Lastly, a driver who is unfamiliar with the car could wind up on the side of the road. If a person who has only ever driven a four-door, economy vehicle gets behind the wheel of a race car, no one will be shocked if they drive right into a ditch.

THE ANALOGY

A car and driver can be analogous to who we are because it represents a separation between our mind and our brain. Who I am is *not* my brain. Who I am *is* my mind. My brain is tangible, but my mind is *intangible*.

For example, what was the first cause of any building you see? It was an idea! Someone first had to have an intangible idea brought into tangible form as a drawing. It could then be executed to produce the tangible benefit we all see: the finished building.

The intangible me interacts with the world through my brain, which leads to my behavior depending on the circumstances. In this analogy, my brain is the vehicle through which I take in and experience sensory information, and then I decide how I react to my surroundings. In essence, I am the driver. The *Intangible Driver*. My brain is the car. I can operate my car the wrong way, run it into the ground within a few decades and cause damage to other cars. Or, I can operate my car well, and it can run efficiently and effectively for a century.

At Flowcess, we help people learn how to keep their cars on the road (which we refer to as "Resiliency") and how to operate their cars at peak performance (the ultimate state of vibrant mental health, which we call "Flow").

We help people fix internal mechanical issues, such as dealing with trauma or bad habits. And, we help people learn how to handle external circumstances such as other drivers or unexpected terrains.

To become an excellent driver of your car and know how to care for your car, you need to identify your driver and understand the car you own and operate. All of this begins with the driver of the car. Your uniqueness!

Each of us was born with a specific uniqueness, a driver that never changes. Who you were as a toddler is the same uniqueness you are today. Your car and your ability to drive it are determined by the skills you've gained or not gained through all the understanding and experience you've accumulated over your lifetime.

Our opportunity is to learn how to drive our cars at their maximum potential and feel alive and energized. Or we can drive it right into a ditch and feel unfulfilled and miserable.

Our driver and car are first affected by our parents, family, and early caretakers. If your driver conflicts with your parent's driver, this could result in you experiencing trauma or trying to intentionally act differently to get along with others. If that happened, it would be like that person who owns a four-door, economy car getting behind the wheel of a race car. It's not going to end well.

The first step we take with our clients is to identify their driver apart from their car. Every other test focuses on your behavior. They assume that it must result from who you are and then try to get the answer by looking more closely at you. This approach values your external circumstances more than your intrinsic motivation. Worse, we've seen personality tests say who you are *is* your behavior when you are stressed. At Flowcess, we look away from you to see the effect you most want to help others experience! Through years of research on the most leading-edge neuroscience, we show that who you are is separate from your behaviors because behaviors are dependent on external circumstances.

I am Jonathan. I drive a sedan. If I skid when I leave the parking lot, what would you think of people who call me "Skid"? I'm not Skid. I'm Jonathan. Skid is my behavior when I'm unbalanced due to external circumstances. This is what personality tests measure.

What would you think of someone who called me "Sedan"? I'm not Sedan. I'm Jonathan. Sedan is my brain. This is what occurs when people say a person is ADHD or bipolar.

Not only am I Jonathan, but with the Flowcess information we are sharing, others would instantly be able to tell when I'm "not myself" when I'm driving my sedan, based on the intentions I have towards others. If others understand my uniqueness, they will know when I'm not driving my sedan properly.

Before we cover the intrinsic motivation of the intangible you, two additional measures of uniqueness characterize how people like to drive their car. Many personality tests also confuse these with who the person is, so we want to address them separately to help you focus on the intangible you.

PICTURE PERSPECTIVE

Have you ever heard that people are either right-brained or left-brained? They are referring to two lobes in our brain. The picture perspective comes from the right lobe and left lobe of our brain. For a long time, scientists thought that these two lobes were split according to logic and creativity. However, this was disproved a long time ago. The two lobes have to do with how big or small of a perspective you have on the world around you. The right lobe is a Big Picture perspective, and the left lobe is a Small Picture perspective.

When we begin a thought, we start it on one side of the brain and use the other side to check it or confirm it. If our thought begins on the right side, we would say that it is "Big Picture," or more abstract and concerned with the connections between facts. If we begin on the left side of the brain, we would say it is "Small Picture," which is more detailed and focused on the facts themselves.

If we look at this in terms of our car and driver analogy, we could say that Big Picture people are looking down the road. They're looking for their exit, and they'll never miss it because they've spotted it from a mile away. However, they aren't paying attention to the road directly in front of their car, and they hit every single pothole.

A Small Picture person is the opposite. They'll be focused on the road directly in front of them. They're looking for potholes or speed bumps, or they're dodging birds and squirrels like it's their job. And it might take them ten minutes to realize they missed their exit.

Picture perspective is on a spectrum. An extremely Big Picture person is getting to their destination, but they will grind out their suspension by catching air on a speed bump. An extremely Small Picture person will keep their car in pristine condition for years by avoiding any damaging collision, but they will miss every turn and never wind up where they're trying to go.

Everyone can think Big or Small Picture. What we are looking for is the *direction* a person tends to go to get energy. For example, when I say "dog," do you tend to think about the dog's location and what is surrounding it (Big Picture)? Or do you tend to think of the breed of the dog and wonder what its name might be (Small Picture)?

How Big or Small Picture a person is will be unique to each individual. Someone can be bigger picture than another person who is Big Picture. Someone can be smaller picture than another person who is also Small Picture. This is the first measure for how people like to drive their car. It is the simplest for people to apply and see immediate results.

PROCESSING PERSPECTIVE

The other measure is how someone processes information. Again, there are two options: External and Internal.

We like to say Internal Processors tend to "think to talk," while External Processors "talk to think."

This is a crucial point to the model because of how it relates to decision-making. When an Internal Processor states a decision, they mean it. It is final, and if you treat it like they haven't made up their mind, they will have a negative experience.

When an External Processor states their decision, they mean that they are considering that option and need to state options out loud a few different ways before they are settled and ready to move on.

In our car and driver analogy, an Internal Processor is like a driver in New York City. They've decided they are going to merge, they turn their blinker on, and they are going whether you are in the way or not. So move and let them in because they've made their decision.

An External Processor is more like a Midwest driver. They realize they need to get in the right lane to take their exit, so they turn on their blinker and then look behind them to see if any car is in the way. They see a driver, and they say, "Well, are you going to let me in or not?" When an External Processor states their will, it means that a negotiation has begun!

When we've helped teachers identify the students' processing perspective, we ask all the Internal Processors to stand up, and the whole room is silent. After they sit down, we ask the External Processors to stand up, and every single one of them starts talking. "Well, I guess I'm supposed to stand up now." "Why are we standing up?" "I'll just move my chair back and stand up."

Afterward, we look at all the Internal Processors sitting down and say, "See? They can't even stand up without talking." Everyone laughs because the Internal Processors struggle to understand why the External Processors talk all the time, and the External Processors feel understood because they struggle to do anything without talking at the same time.

In Section 2, we will cover applications for both of these measures that personality tests tend to confuse with the intangible you. For now, let's focus on determining your Intangible Driver!

THE INTANGIBLE DRIVER®

Have you ever started a diet with a solid determination to succeed, only to give up after a few days? Who you are, your driver, wanted to do something, but it had to work through your brain, your car, to accomplish the goal. Something went wrong between your desire and the behavior that resulted from trying to get something accomplished through your brain and how others responded. Your brain manages your behavior, and you may not see it because you are focused on your intention.

It's as if you were driving a car that continuously veered to one side. Would you immediately think something was wrong with you, the driver, or would you think something was wrong with the car, or would you think something is wrong with the road? You would naturally think something was wrong with the car, and you would take it to a mechanic, where they would determine that your wheel alignment is off.

However, if you don't take it to the mechanic, you will spend a lot of time and effort trying to keep the car moving in the right direction. And if you take your eyes off of it for a moment, you'll end up hitting another vehicle or running off the road. Regardless, the mechanic isn't going to try to fix *you*. They know the car is the issue.

At Flowcess, we know that operating according to your uniqueness results in energy and feeling settled or valued, meaning it *feels right*. It is an intrinsic motivation. We also identify the behaviors that align with and result from your uniqueness, as well as behaviors that operate against your uniqueness, regardless of your circumstances.

This separates you from your behaviors. We've found this helps people feel more in control over their actions because they can intentionally act according to who they are to gain energy and motivation regardless of the situation and circumstance.

Once you can control your car, you can direct that energy towards situations that require more effort, such as situations you don't *want* to step into or you know might exhaust you. Instead of only being able to get motivated and energized by chance or realizing you are about to gain or lose something, you can get energy intentionally and in healthy ways.

We have helped numerous people make it through situations and surroundings that used to trigger or drain them by helping them understand how their uniqueness is hindered or knocked off the road by careless drivers. We will see how each Intangible Driver has a behavior that the individual believes is wrong only because of how others have responded to it.

I went through this for years. When I was touring the country in a rock band, I was running away from feeling alone, so I turned to fame, drugs, and women to make me happy. Instead, I felt empty and depressed experiencing these external circumstances. I was told I was weak for focusing on peoples' feelings. It wasn't until years later when I learned who I am, that I realized that I was doing everything in opposition to what gives me energy and joy. All the things that my "friends" told me were supposed to be fun and enjoyable were making me miserable, and I had no idea why.

Learning my Intangible Driver taught me that I could get energy intentionally by being more myself regardless of my circumstances. I love helping people to relieve their pain. When I get to help someone in a rough spot, and they tell me, "I feel better, Jonathan," I feel like I thought I would when performing in front of thousands of fans.

How was I supposed to get energy from such a wild life? I never did. I *do* get energy from being myself, and when I look back on all of those musicians I used to work with, I feel sorry for them. So many of them are still trying to chase that dream, convinced that it just takes more fame, more money, and more women to make them happy. I don't know one of them still chasing that dream who is as happy and energized as I am now.

Now let's discover the driver of your car!

THE QUIZ

Identifying your Intangible Driver is crucial to getting the most out of this book. *Please* don't skip this step.

We use an online quiz to help our clients determine their Intangible Driver. You can find the quiz here: flowcess.com/intangible-driver

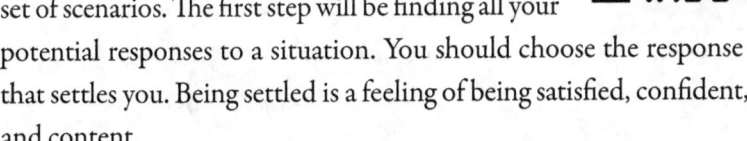

The quiz guides you through a straightforward set of scenarios. The first step will be finding all your potential responses to a situation. You should choose the response that settles you. Being settled is a feeling of being satisfied, confident, and content.

Your focus should be to try to imagine the scenario and answer the question as honestly as possible. You should not choose the answer based on what you feel is the proper or moral way others would want you to respond. None of the responses are right or wrong. You simply want to choose the response that is most likely the one you would do.

Don't be concerned with having too many options at first because we will be eliminating options until we are left with only one or two. You will be given a few examples for you to look at for each step so that you can follow along more easily. This quiz will be *contrastive*, meaning it will determine who you are and confirm who you are not.

Please go to flowcess.com/intangible-driver, take the quiz, then go on to the next chapter.

CHAPTER 2

INTANGIBLE DRIVERS®

When I discover who I am, I'll be free.
—Ralph Ellison

BEFORE I LEARNED my Intangible Driver, I relied on my experiences to teach me what I got energy from and what motivated me. So I needed many, many experiences to start to form trends. It took years and many painful interactions to articulate that I wanted to help people grow by helping them deal with the pain in their lives. If I had known my ID earlier, I could have avoided years of bad decisions trying to figure out who I was and could have intentionally been helping others. I could have avoided the bad feelings I felt from others not being able to handle my uniqueness. When I listen to old songs that I wrote, I can hear someone struggling to find who they are.

You are now on the path to finding the true you. The Intangible You. That person you have been searching for all your life. The person you have bumped into here and there. When you operate a certain way, it just clicks, and you feel amazing: **the Intangible You**.

Now that you've determined your Intangible Driver, this chapter will give you a big picture overview of each ID before digging deeper into the upcoming chapters. The seven Intangible Drivers are:

Perceiver
Teacher
Compassion
Giver
Server
Administrator
Exhorter

PERCEIVER

Perceiver IDs want to make others aware of issues. As soon as they walk into a room, they instantly see three to five wrong things without even trying. They tend to focus on the past. They feel settled and valued when others say they see what is being pointed out. People can see Perceivers as highly negative and pessimistic because they often point out issues and problems and have a hard time letting those go until others are aware.

The response of "You dropped your ice cream" is a Perceiver response. When Perceivers take the quiz and hear that response, they usually laugh or try to make me aware that it would be stupid to say that response. Comedians are generally Perceivers. If you see something wrong and just can't help but point it out, then you might be a Perceiver.

TEACHERS

Teacher IDs want to research and explain the reasons. We say that Perceivers are focused on a what, while Teachers are focused on a why. Teachers consistently ask why and often can't help but explain the reason, even if no one asked. Teachers are also past-focused, though if you look at a spectrum from past to future, Teachers are not as past-focused as Perceivers. They feel settled and valued when someone shows they understand, and they love to see that light go on in someone's eyes—the aha moment. Teachers can be seen as know-it-alls because they share or explain information on seemingly any topic, also known as commentating.

The response of, "You dropped your sundae because it wasn't balanced on the plate," is a Teacher response. Notice, they respond the same as a Perceiver, plus add some commentary. However, they are focused on giving understanding, while a Perceiver just wants to make others aware. When I tell jokes to my Teacher friends, I always explain why it's funny, and the Teachers laugh harder! If you can't help but explain the why, even if no one is still listening, you might be a Teacher.

COMPASSION

Compassion IDs have a natural propensity for empathy. "Compassionators," as I like to call them, want to relieve emotional pain, and they do that by feeling the emotional pain of others.

Many people are empathetic, but Compassion IDs naturally feel what others feel and cannot help it. Compassions are misunderstood as being weak because we only see the effects of them feeling others' pain. If I'm with my friend who is not Compassion, and we both get hurt, he feels his own pain, but I feel his pain and my pain. I get double the pain! If it's bad enough, I might cry, and the people who see us would think he's strong and I am weak.

However, Compassion is the strongest ID because they are *always* bearing the pain for other people. They help others work through their pain by bearing it while the other person focuses on fixing the issue or moving past the pain.

The response of, "Don't feel bad, it could have happened to anyone," is the Compassion response. Individuals who are Compassion instantly know who is in pain when they walk into a room. Just like Perceivers can't help but notice when things are off, Compassionators can't help but feel the pain from others.

Compassion IDs want others to share their emotions with them because they like to feel what other people feel and can relieve their pain. If it hurts when others say, "You're causing me pain!" then you might be Compassion.

GIVER

Giver IDs want to provide a tangible need and make improvements. Commonly, Givers are the ones who will offer money or tangible items to make a situation better. While giving something tangible is the most common way to identify a Giver, they are focused on the improvement. They will offer anything they can to make that improvement, including a good idea or plan.

If a Giver tries to give and is shut down or rejected, they will feel unsettled and not valued. The easiest way to help a Giver feel good is to let them give to you. Notice that doesn't mean you should take advantage of them and ask them for money or material goods. It means that when they offer you something, receive it and thank them. A Giver just wants to be appreciated.

The response of, "Let me buy you another sundae," is the Giver response. Giver is unique. While the previous three IDs are focused on the past, and the next three on the future, a Giver is focused on the present. A side effect of this is that Givers can seem unemotional because they are only going to express the emotion they are feeling in this moment. A Perceiver might still feel angry over something they saw a month ago and keep a fresh, expressive scowl on their face, while a Giver wouldn't express it because once the moment is over, they don't feel it any longer. If you get frustrated or mad when people refuse your gifts or offers to improve things, you might be a Giver.

SERVERS

Servers want to provide for the needs. While the Giver wants to buy you another sundae, the Server wants to help you clean up the sundae that fell, and they won't feel settled if there is still a mess. A Server seeks to fill a need for someone else, and they will adjust their response to however the situation requires them to fill that need.

A Giver wants to make something good even better, while a Server wants to fix something that isn't good. While all the other IDs are static, the Server is fluid. They will act like any of the other IDs, as needed to get the need filled. This results in some interesting dynamics. Servers can be seen as having no personality, chameleons, or being fake around different people because they adjust to the situation. Servers are a forward-focused ID, and they have a hard time focusing on their own needs.

The response of, "Let me help you clean that up!" is a Server response. Servers are focused on the future. They want to fill the needs of other people and not their own, resulting in procrastination with their own needs. A common trait of Servers is that they'll spend hours cleaning up a friend's house and feel energized, but just the thought of cleaning their own house drains them completely. If you are the first one to jump to your feet when others share a need, or you need to learn to say no when people ask for help, or you instantly stop wanting to do something when I tell you that you *have to* do it, you might be a Server.

ADMINISTRATOR

Administrators want to direct a group towards a goal. While a Server or Compassion is focused on an individual, an Administrator is focused on the group and the space and distance in between. This could be the distance between two people in the group or the distance between a person and their goal. Administrators feel energized when they get to direct a group. However, if the Administrator doesn't have a goal, they can become stagnant and unmotivated. The easiest way to motivate an Administrator is to tell them your goal or give them a goal that challenges them.

The response of, "Kurt, grab a mop. Jenny, help Andrew with the tray. Tom, get Andrew a new sundae," is an Administrator response. They are focused on the future. Perceivers usually get in trouble in school because they can't help but push an issue until someone sees what they see. Administrators are the kids who get in trouble, not because they did something, but because they got a bunch of other kids to do something.

If you are listless when you don't have a goal or see people as just part of a group instead of on the individual level, you might be an Administrator.

EXHORTER

Exhorters are the final ID and are the most forward or future-focused. Exhorters want to encourage others towards the future. More specifically, an Exhorter wants to move forward and gets excited thinking about moving forward. While Compassionators want to feel what other people are feeling, Exhorters want other people to feel what they are feeling. It is common for Exhorters to be misunderstood as conceited or narcissistic because they are so focused on how *they* feel that it seems like the world revolves around them. They are also misunderstood as empty-headed cheerleaders or dreamers because they want other people to feel excited, and they are running forward towards the future.

The response of, "Next time we'll sit at the counter, so this won't happen," is an Exhorter response. Exhorters are always looking to the future, and they believe that if others felt what they felt, then everyone

would be able to move forward. A side effect of Exhorters progressing things forward is they can easily get into fear about something in the future. Something small that is years away can seem huge and right now.

If you get irrationally afraid about minor things or get frustrated when others don't feel what you feel, you might be an Exhorter.

WHY AND HOW

Your Intangible Driver is made up of two parts. It's called your WHY and your HOW.

Your WHY is the *reason* you do something. It's the effect you want others to experience and the source of you growing in energy. Your HOW is the *way* you do something. It's the method you want to use to connect with others.

Think of restaurants. Why do they exist? What effect do they want to have on people? Some restaurants want people to be efficiently fed. Some want people to connect with family and friends. Some want people to experience other cultures.

Determining this reason would be determining the restaurant's WHY. The unique way they achieve this WHY is through their HOW.

It's HOW they help people achieve the WHY. HOW one restaurant might reach and connect with people is through fast food service, another through a street stand, and another through a private chef.

All of us have a unique way of WHY we want to interact with others and a unique way of HOW we interact with others, just like how one restaurant might serve people through a street stand (HOW) so that people can be efficiently fed (WHY).

I am a Compassion-Server. I want to connect with others by filling their needs (HOW) so that I can bear their pain or help them not feel bad (WHY).

Since our HOW is the first connection we experience with a person, we can think that a person's HOW is the reason WHY they are interacting. This is one reason many of us feel misunderstood, especially if our HOW and WHY IDs are far apart. If the people I interact with only see me as a Server, they won't understand that what I really desire is to bear their pain. I'd never feel settled. I'd never feel known or understood.

But since I know my Intangible Driver and I know my WHY and HOW, I can intentionally help others be aware of the best way to interact with me. Soon, you will be able to do the same!

In the following chapters, we will take an in-depth look at each Intangible Driver. You will be guided on this journey by some of my friends and colleagues who have mastered their uniqueness. The objective is for you to understand yourself. We have included tips and information that can help you become a better version of yourself, a better driver.

We also outline how to interact with each of the IDs to help you have better interactions and more profound and meaningful relationships. You'll be able to see what drivers you more naturally get along with and why you might experience more tension with other drivers. The second section of this book consists of greater applications resulting from understanding your uniqueness and the uniqueness of others.

Feel free to jump ahead to the chapters that are relevant to you, or simply start at the beginning with Perceiver. Either way, I encourage you to read all of the chapters because understanding each ID will help you interact with all people.

The goal is to understand who you are and begin your personal growth journey that will lead to vibrant mental health, more satisfying relationships, and unassailable happiness.

Let's begin!

CHAPTER 3

PERCEIVER

"You dropped your sundae."

I'D LIKE to introduce you to a friend of mine, Simon.

Simon is a Perceiver, and because our IDs shape the way we view the world and how we interact with others, Simon will always help me see something I wouldn't have on my own. I love spending time with Simon because his observations are so funny and have me on the floor laughing. He is also great at pointing out issues in my life which helps me grow as a person.

Perceivers like to point out facts to make others aware. The Perceiver's response in the ice cream quiz is, "You dropped your sundae."

Simon will help us better grasp what it's like to be a Perceiver and what it's like to interact with a Perceiver.

Simon, what is your story?

GROWING UP

Growing up, my father was an alcoholic. I remember watching it grow as a problem from the time I was a toddler until I was nine years old. I remember seeing from other people's parents around me that this wasn't how a father was supposed to act. I also remember hearing my brother and mom discussing how worried they were becoming over my dad's drinking. However, they were afraid to say anything to him. They didn't want to confront him.

We would always find him in the morning passed out in his truck or on the couch. As things got worse, I watched as my brother's anger grew, and he held it inside. My mother kept bearing more and more of the burden left behind from the weight my dad was no longer carrying in the marriage.

They were afraid to say anything, and I remember being unable to keep my mouth shut.

They might have thought I was stupid, brave, or both, but at nine years old, I was standing toe to toe with my dad and telling him every single thing he was doing that was destroying our family—face to face, son to father, boy to man.

Anytime I've been in trouble in my life, that seems to have been the reason. When I notice something is wrong, I can't help myself. It's like there's a burning inside until I finally blurt it out. I need someone to see what I'm seeing.

Unfortunately, this has often been seen as negative to many people in my life, even though I am actually trying to make a situation better or help someone!

Discovering that I'm a Perceiver was a relief. My entire life, I've moved between feeling like I'm a terrible person for constantly feeling the need to point out everything wrong, to feeling like everyone else was an idiot for not seeing it for themselves. It wasn't a fun way to live.

When I learned that I'm a Perceiver, it helped me understand that I had a natural inclination to see the facts and just the facts. I'm not distracted by the feelings, the reasons, or the future. I just see the facts, and that allows me to pinpoint when something is wrong. Sometimes it feels obnoxious. Like when I walk into a room and say, "This wall is a different color than the rest of the room."

I have a friend who likes to respond to my statements with, "Thanks, Captain Obvious."

But that same friend will bring me along on important meetings when he needs to know if someone is being truthful or lying. In those moments, it feels like a superpower. It feels like I can see, without any effort or thought, every little fact that a person is misquoting. It is instant, and most of the people around me aren't able to see it. Finding out that I'm a Perceiver allowed me to recognize my superpower and realize that the people around me aren't dumb. They just aren't Perceivers. They need someone like me in their life.

I used to feel so frustrated with my friends when they didn't see what I saw. Now, I'm happy that I get to help them see, even if it is still annoying. They miss some of the most obvious facts, and I feel fantastic helping them see them.

Discovering my Intangible Driver did illuminate why I naturally found myself wanting to point out what seemed so obvious to me! It explained why I spent so much time frustrated when it seemed like other people weren't seeing the same issues that I was. It's because they weren't! Understanding that fact has helped my marriage, family, friendships, and work relationships. Not only do I understand what I do best, but also what it is that I don't do best. I have learned to value others for their strengths, as well.

WHO AM I

As a Perceiver, I want to make people aware of a fact. Perceivers will state a fact and only the fact so that you are aware of that fact. The easiest way to recognize a fact is that it is the answer to a *what* question. For example, *what happened*, *what is that*, or *what was said*. This is different from Teachers who answer *why* questions, as in *why did that happen*.

A Perceiver will not be settled or feel valued until someone is aware. Most of my stories about Perceivers deal with this point. This may be the student in class that repeats themselves over and over or the husband who accuses his wife of never listening to him. They were simply looking for someone to acknowledge what they see.

Perceivers easily see everything, especially when things are wrong, and they tend to think everyone sees things just as easily. If you are a Perceiver, this is one misconception that can help you have better relationships. The value you offer is seeing things that are wrong or off before anyone else. I know that I can feel like other people are stupid or oblivious, but in reality, it's a value that Perceivers can see these things first and then share them with others.

On top of that benefit, think of your favorite joke. Nine times out of ten, a good joke is just someone pointing out a fact.

"You don't need a parachute to go skydiving. You need a parachute to go skydiving twice."

Even when I explain what a Perceiver does, it draws a laugh. Pointing things out can be funny. It is what comedians do for a living, and the best comedians are Perceivers. We want to make people aware of something. Anything. We aren't settled until we feel convinced you see what we see. And a laugh is proof they saw it. Do you see?! ...seriously, though.

CONFIRMATION QUESTIONS

Without trying, when you enter a room, do you instantly see three to five things that are off? Do you feel settled when others confirm they see what you see? Do you state a lot of *what's* by just pointing things out?

Do you think you are a Perceiver? Do you know someone who might be a Perceiver?

DIRECTION

Perceivers are focused on the past because something had to exist already for them to perceive it. They are infinitely focused on the past because as they think about the fact, they can connect it to another fact that occurred even further back in time. They get energy by looking further and further into the past.

A Perceiver could be thinking about something that happened at work the day before and jump further backward in their thoughts to how they were in that job because of the choice they made in their college degree, and then jump further backward to remember a conversation they had with a teacher in the second grade that led them to pursue the college degree, and so on.

Ever since I got my drivers' license, one of my favorite things to do has been to put on some music that I associate with specific periods of my life and drive through the streets I grew up on, past the houses I lived in as a child during that period. I get energized by reflecting on the past. For my entire life, I have been looking to the past to make sense of the present. The older I get and the more memories I make, the longer and more frequent these drives become.

As a Perceiver, I am constantly taking in the world through the lens of things that have already occurred. Once I realized this, it explained my fondness for seemingly pointless drives and helped make sense of the tension that can arise with others who tend to be more future-focused.

METHOD

What do I like to do when I'm on vacation? As I have gotten older, I have started using my free time, like vacations, to start doing the things that I haven't had time to do or enough time to do.

While my wife and I were vacationing in Europe, I found that the longer we were there, the more relaxed I got as I began to get in the flow of things. Pretty soon, I found myself waking up early to walk to corner cafes and write every morning. I know, crazy, right? Most people on vacation like to sleep in and relax by not doing anything! The weird thing is, I never really wrote before that trip.

For me, I discovered that writing is just one unique way for me to perceive. Writing allows me to articulate what I see and then mold and refine it until it is just right. More importantly, it provides me with a clear avenue to precisely express my thoughts and document them.

You know what I didn't do on that vacation? I didn't start trying to organize things, fix things, or do as many things as possible in as little time as possible. I wrote, and I enjoyed good food, good wine, and good espresso.

I came home from that vacation feeling like I accomplished something, like I discovered something in myself. I realized that as a Perceiver, I prefer to *say* things and not *do* things. It energizes me to share my observations. Spending a significant amount of time on my vacation writing led to the trip being my best vacation ever.

THE WHY EFFECT

Remember, a person can be a Perceiver in their WHY, or their HOW, or both. In the WHY, the effect a Perceiver wants is for others to be aware of a fact. They are not settled and don't feel valued until you see it.

I live in a weird part of my state. At least I think it's weird. But I am a Perceiver.

A couple of weeks ago, my wife and I were driving to play tennis at the park. As we drove through one of the neighborhoods, I noticed a squat, rectangular-shaped house, followed by a towering Victorian home, followed by a tri-level from the mid-seventies. I abruptly turned to my wife and said, "Where do we live?!" It was too much for me. All the different types of homes crunched together in the same block did not make sense to me at all.

A week later, some friends were in town visiting. We were driving through the same neighborhood, and as we drove past the same houses, my friend said out loud, "These houses are weird!" Yes! Someone else sees it! Sweet release! That's the moment I live for. I had a boost of energy and felt so good because all I want is for you to see what I see. And my friend did!

I ask people constantly after I share an observation, "Do you know what I mean?" My friends now feel plagued by that question because I ask it on repeat without any effort. But I do so for a particular reason. *I need to know if you see what I see.* Do you see what I see?

THE HOW CONNECTION

When someone is a Perceiver in their HOW, they want to make people aware of the fact. They connect with others by stating the facts.

I'm a Perceiver-Perceiver, both the WHY and the HOW, so what you see is what you get, but my friend Ben is an Administrator-Perceiver. His objective is always to move a group towards a goal, and HOW he does that is by perceiving. But when he perceives, he *feels* like he has done everything necessary to get that group moving. Perceiving is his unique way of connecting with others, so when he does it, it feels like he has given all he can to connect.

A Perceiver WHY wouldn't feel settled just stating the fact and moving on. We want the effect to be that you are aware of the fact. It is WHY we perceive.

Ben is a musician, and if he's playing with a group of musicians, he'll perceive by pointing something out, like the lack of tension in a song. He might say, "Hey guys, this song is too bland. It needs more tension."

Ben feels like he's done everything he needs to do to get the group to play the song better. He tried to connect with them by perceiving, which was through his Perceiver-HOW. He perceived to get the effect he wanted, which was for the band to play the song using more tension: his Administrator-WHY. The band saw Ben perceiving. It's what they felt. It was the connection between Ben and the band. But WHY Ben perceived wasn't to make them aware of a fact. He wanted them to move towards the goal of making the music more intense.

When we are interacting with others, we see or feel their HOW Intangible Driver first. It's *how* we connect with each other. But the reason they are connecting with us can be for a different reason. The effect they want us to have is through their WHY Intangible Driver. It is *why* they are interacting with us.

If the band members don't know Ben, they might completely miss what he truly was trying to do.

If you have watched Sherlock Holmes, this helps explain why he can be such a struggle to get along with. Sherlock is a Teacher-Perceiver.

He wants to point out facts (perceive) so that other people understand (teach), and when he points out a fact, he feels like he's said everything necessary for other people to understand to the same level that he does.

In most Sherlock stories, upon first meeting his client, he makes a few casual remarks about their personal life, "I observe that you are a banker by trade, that things have not been going well with your wife, and that you've had great success recently. What are you here to see me about?"

The client is astounded. How could he know these things?

Sherlock's response is sometimes gentle, "It is simplicity itself," and occasionally crass, "It would take a blind man to miss it."

Sherlock will point out three facts at a crime scene and remark at how empty-headed everyone else must be when they don't instantly come to the same conclusion that he has because Sherlock feels like he's explained by just pointing out the fact. When asked to elaborate, he becomes annoyed and begins to explain everything directly.

He is annoyed because, as a Teacher-Perceiver, he just wants to state the fact to connect with people, which is his Perceiver-HOW. He feels the effect of stating the fact is that you should understand the reason, which is his Teacher-WHY. He isn't connecting through Teaching, so if his facts don't help the person understand, it will drain him of energy to have to give understanding. He just wants the effect to be that you understand.

MISUNDERSTOOD

Most people misunderstand Perceivers as being extremely negative and pessimistic. Many Perceivers have suffered a lot of unnecessary abuse beginning in their childhood, especially during their middle school years. When they attempted to make other people aware, their classmates would respond with comments such as, "Why do you always have to be so negative?" or "Thank you, Captain Obvious!"

The classmates often responded this way because they were insecure and couldn't handle the tension of having something wrong pointed out to them. A parent might have reinforced this with comments such as, "If you can't say anything nice, don't say anything at all."

The Perceivers who experienced this may begin to believe they are negative people and will not share their observations out of fear that they could be a bad person. However, one can only hold themselves back for so long, and when they can't hold back anymore, it tends to be something they feel strongly about. Because of this, they end up acting out in very argumentative or explosive ways, even destroying relationships.

An example I have as a Perceiver of feeling misunderstood is in a professional setting. As a Perceiver, I tend to naturally want to bring attention to things that aren't perfect and things that could or should be better. If someone is insecure or too immature to handle me doing this, I have found that they will tend to lash out at me. I will often find out that they felt like what I was saying was something personal towards them when what I was saying probably had nothing to do with them at all. I have even been called very mean names for acting in my ID.

If you have a lot of interactions with a Perceiver, the easiest way to help them is to confirm that you see what they are trying to make you aware of by saying, "I see." If you have many arguments with a Perceiver, it might be because you don't say, "I see." when they point something out. Saying or doing anything other than showing that you are aware will cause the Perceiver to remain misunderstood, and they will feel like they still need to make you aware. In fact, if they have had trauma in this area, they might start fighting with you immediately if you don't say that you see.

Six out of the seven Intangible Drivers don't really care that much if you don't see what they see. One of the seven will experience pain if you don't at least acknowledge what they are pointing out. You don't have to agree with them. You don't have to tell them that they are right. Just tell them that you see it.

Dave, a good friend of mine, used to take his Perceiver wife, Stephanie, to work every day. On the way, they would stop at a grocery store to get her a salad for lunch. One day they arrived early, and the salad bar wasn't open. Stephanie looked in disbelief, walking back and forth next to the salad bar. Finally, she looked at Dave and said, in outrage, "The salad bar isn't open yet!"

Dave, an expert at interacting successfully with Perceivers, responded by saying, "The salad bar *isn't* open yet!"

His comment showed her that he saw what she saw. He even put an extra inflection on the 'isn't' to reinforce that he understood. How do you think she responded?

She laughed!

Dave knows Stephanie is a Perceiver, and he wants to help her feel known. He intentionally responds by repeating what she states back to her, even adding inflections so that she feels like he sees. This actually causes her to feel safe.

Another friend was there at the time, and after Stephanie walked away laughing, the friend asked, "Why didn't you...?" "Why didn't I what?" Dave asked, "Why didn't I ask her what she wanted me to do about it? Why didn't I push back?"

Dave explained to his friend that if he pushed back in that moment instead of showing that he was aware, his wife would feel unsettled. She wouldn't suddenly apologize for being rude; she would start to perceive on him instead! Now, instead of laughing and feeling good, Dave would have been the catalyst to his wife getting upset and, potentially, making both of them have a terrible day!

UNHEALTHY USE OF ID

Every Intangible Driver is a strength and value but can be misused if the person is in a bad place mentally or emotionally. It happens when people have trauma or damage in an area or they feel unstable or unsafe.

For Perceivers, this misuse can come out as a dictator. The Perceiver will state a *what* that implies that you should do what he says because he said so; no reason is shared. Joseph Stalin said, "Death is the solution to all problems. No man – no problem." He stated a *what*, as a matter of fact, without regard to any reasoning if it is moral or not.

Further, some Perceivers go so far that they believe they see something that isn't real. We call this belief divination. For example, a mother who is a Perceiver may enter a room and see her latest fashion magazine torn to pieces. She immediately blames her two-year-old son without any inquiry. She saw a situation and felt correct, settled, and confident to jump to the conclusion.

Later, when reviewing a baby cam set up in the room, she sees that it was actually the dog that tore up the magazine.

Whenever I've struggled in my life as a Perceiver, it has been because I've firmly decided that whatever I say is inherently factual. It's right. I know it's right because the things that I say are right. I convince myself that the facts that I see are the facts of reality. When I'm struggling with that state of mind, others often don't like dealing with me. No matter what someone says, if I feel someone is wrong, I feel compelled to tell them they're wrong, even if my facts aren't correct.

It has manifested in different ways over the years. I've convinced myself that some future event that *might* transpire *will* transpire, like a plane I'm on crashing. I've decided for myself what someone's intentions are and then treated them according to the decision that I made inside my head. Anytime I've made myself the source of the fact, instead of relying on the facts themselves, I've been massively wrong and hurt myself and my friends.

RELATIONSHIPS

Perceivers get along well with Compassion IDs. Compassion wants to relieve pain. When perceiving occurs, others often feel pain as they become aware of issues. Realizing they've made a mistake and beginning to make changes can hurt! People who are Compassion like to help relieve the pain for those who are making changes in their lives. Likewise, Perceivers often get a lot of pushback and are the subject of misunderstandings.

If the Compassion person realizes the Perceiver is just trying to help, they would want to bear that pain. If you are Compassion, this is an opportunity to help Perceivers by realizing that they are trying to help. If you are a Perceiver, share what you are trying to achieve when you perceive with the Compassion people in your life. This way, they understand that you aren't trying to cause pain; you're trying to get problems addressed so that those issues don't cause more significant problems down the road.

Perceivers often get along with Administrator IDs. Administrators want to organize a group of people to accomplish some kind of goal. Administrators feel like they can achieve anything if they only knew the reality of the situation. Perceivers are reality junkies and will happily tell the Administrator everything they need to know. If you are an Administrator, you'll be able to get a lot more done if you look for and listen to the Perceivers in your life. If you are a Perceiver, you can explain who you are and how your perceiving can help the Administrator facilitate a person or group of people towards a goal.

Exhorter IDs tend to avoid Perceivers. Exhorters want people to be encouraged, and it feels like the worst possible situation for them when someone is discouraged. When we go through the quiz and give the Perceiver option, "You dropped your sundae," Perceivers tend to laugh. Exhorters will make a disgusted face and ask, "Who would say something like that?"

CAREERS

Often, successful comedians are Perceivers because their goal is to make you aware. When we get words to our feelings about a conflict, contradiction, or injustice, it feels funny!

Law enforcement is a very common profession for Perceivers because they need to be observant and skilled at gathering and stating facts.

Manufacturing is another example because details may be missed creating a product, and it is highly valued when someone can point it out on the production floor.

Finally, poets and songwriters are often Perceivers because by just giving the *what*, it allows us to supply our own meaning and emotion to the words. When someone shares too much information in their song, it usually just sounds bad.

As Perceivers grow in their expertise in a particular industry, they can make excellent consultants. After becoming an expert in my field, I was interacting with an owner of another company in the same industry. He, his son, and I were having drinks together, and we began discussing the state of their business and where they thought opportunities could be for growth.

This company was based out of the town I grew up in, and I knew it very well. I knew their business model, and I shared that I had some observations to make if they were willing to hear it, and they were interested.

I shared my observations, and they loved it. It was like I was giving them words to their feelings. I said many things to them that would require a lot of work and were brutal critiques on work they had already done, but they heard it and appreciated it. They recognized the value of my advice, and by the end of the meal, they both hugged me.

CHILDREN: PARENTING AND TEACHING

Research has shown that students who are regularly sent to the principal's office are usually Perceivers.

I recently watched a Perceiver student in a class notice that someone wasn't paying attention in class and pointed them out to the teacher. How often does the teacher acknowledge the Perceiver by saying, "I see."? Rarely! The teacher told the student to mind their own business and then began to ignore the student.

How did this Perceiver respond? At the start of the situation, the Perceiver was focused on the student who wasn't paying attention, and the student was trying to get the teacher to see that problem. When the teacher didn't see it, the Perceiver saw a new issue: teacher didn't care that a student wasn't paying attention. The Perceiver then focused on the new issue they saw and responded, "Wait a minute. Let me get this straight. You're a teacher, and you don't *care* that a student isn't paying attention? The school pays you to teach us, and you don't *care* about doing your job? That means you're stealing from the school!"

Do you think the teacher told the Perceiver, "I see" at this point? Of course not. The teacher sent the Perceiver to the principal. How do you think the Perceiver responded to this escalating situation? He said, "Of course I'll go to the principal! I want to go to the principal, so I can tell him that he has a teacher in his school who is *stealing* from him!"

Understanding Intangible Drivers has empowered teachers to just respond to a Perceiver by telling them that they see. The situation remains contained and mitigates any escalation.

A few years back, I worked with the president of a local company who had a Perceiver daughter. Whenever they would travel together to work or school, they would end up having arguments.

The daughter would point out the window at a car, let's say a yellow Volkswagen, and say, "That's a yellow Volkswagen."

Her father always wanted to teach her, so he would respond by saying something like, "That yellow is five shades darker than the yellow used on Ford cars!" As soon as he would say anything other than saying he was aware or saw what she was pointing out, she would get upset and start perceiving many issues. That would cause him to be frustrated as well. He would fire back, and they would have a senseless argument.

Once he understood that his daughter was a Perceiver, he started acknowledging that he saw when she perceived. It led to wonderful conversations and bonding. She felt like her dad understood her. After recognizing her perceiving, he could share whatever he wanted, and she would hear him. He no longer has senseless arguments with her.

SELF HELP

If you are a Perceiver, an area that you can grow in that will positively affect your relationships is not getting upset at others when they don't see what you are trying to point out. Is it worth all the frustration and arguments?

The key to being a confident Perceiver is to realize that your perceiving is a value! I had a friend on his company's engineering team. They spent months creating a new product that the company had high hopes to outperform the competition. The only problem is that the marketing team made the product name look like a sexual pun. My Perceiver friend was able to point out the issue before it launched. However, the bosses ignored his valuable advice, and the great product became a public relations nightmare. A Perceiver is writing a blank check, and if others don't want to cash it, that's their loss. The company learned the lesson the hard way but now actively seeks out my friend for his thoughts before launching new ideas.

CHEAT SHEET

Perceiver-Perceiver
Wants to make people aware of an issue just to make people aware of the issue. "You dropped your sundae."

Perceiver-Teacher
Wants to help people understand WHY the issue exists to make people aware of the issue. "The sundae wasn't balanced correctly on the plate, and that's why it fell."

Perceiver-Compassion
Wants to bear the emotional pain of people to make them aware of the issue. "Don't feel bad about your sundae falling. It could have happened to anyone."

Perceiver-Giver
Wants to give a tangible gift or improvement to make people aware of an issue. "Let me buy you a sundae to replace the one that fell."

Notable: There is a very well-known fictional person who is a Perceiver-Giver. He gives gifts to people to let them know if they are good or bad. He's even got a list of the people who are naughty or nice. Can you guess?

Specifically, if you're nice, you get presents; if you're naughty, you get coal. It's Santa Claus!

Santa's goal is for you to see what he sees. Look at this Perceiver description: "He sees you when you are sleeping. He knows when you are awake. He knows when you've been bad or good," because there is no in-between with Santa. In fact, being good for goodness sake is stating a "what" as an effect of another "what"! This perfectly describes the Perceiver "because I said so" mentality!

Perceiver-Server
Wants to fill a need to make people aware of the issue. "Let me help you clean up the sundae that fell."

Perceiver-Administrator
Wants to coordinate a group of people to make people aware of an issue. "Let's work together to clean up the sundae that fell."

Perceiver-Exhorter
Wants to encourage people about the future to make people aware of an issue. "Next time, the sundae won't fall because we will eat at the counter."

FAMOUS EXAMPLES OF PERCEIVER-WHYS

Perceiver-Perceiver: Steve Martin (actor/musician), Ricky Gervais (actor/comedian)

Perceiver-Teacher: Don Henley (musician), George Carlin (comedian), Chris Rock (actor/comedian); Hermione Granger (book/movie *Harry Potter*)

Perceiver-Compassion: Richard Pryor (comedian), Gary Shandling (comedian), George Costanza (TV show *Seinfeld*), Larry David (actor/comedian)

Perceiver-Giver: Santa Claus, Bob Newhart (actor/comedian)

Perceiver-Server: Jerry Seinfeld (actor/comedian), Green Arrow (TV Show *Arrow*)

Perceiver-Administrator: Jim Halpert (TV show *The Office*)

Perceiver-Exhorter: Louis CK (comedian), Robin Williams (comedian)

CHAPTER 4

TEACHER

"You dropped your sundae because it wasn't balanced on the plate."

I HOPE YOU all enjoyed getting to know Simon and learning about what it's like to be a Perceiver. I know I learned a ton!

In this chapter, we're going to learn about the Teacher Intangible Driver. When people hear the word Teacher, they think of an educator, and that's not too far off. Just like an educator is trying to help students understand something, a Teacher wants to explain things. Some of the best examples are college professors giving a lecture to a room full of students to explain the reasons and causes behind something.

To talk about what it's like to be a Teacher, I'd like to introduce my friend Joel. Joel is a Teacher-Teacher, and he lives to figure out the reason for something and then explain it. Whenever I get the chance to talk to Joel, I know I'm going to learn something new, and I know we're going to get in-depth on trying to understand whatever topic we're discussing. It's never a wasted moment with Joel because I'm always going to walk away with more understanding, which helps me grow as a person.

I hope you all get as much value out of listening to Joel as I do.

Joel, will you explain who you are to us?

GROWING UP

Hi, I'm Joel, and I'm a Teacher.

I can remember growing up as a Teacher and feeling like a nuisance, without really having the words to explain it. Anytime someone would state a fact, just a simple fact like Simon talked about in the last chapter, I felt the need to give an explanation. If someone mentioned that there were 365 days in a year, I wanted to explain that it's because the earth revolves around the sun. If we had to draw something in art class, I explained why I drew what I drew to everyone. If I was in line getting lunch, I had to explain why I was choosing green beans to the lunch lady. I explained to my mother why playing outside before doing my homework would make me smarter. I was relentless.

"That's because…" was a constant phrase that I uttered, and I would explain reason after reason, giving endless commentary, whether people wanted to listen or not. People called me a know-it-all whenever I opened my mouth, and that hurt. I was excited that I got to explain things, it gave me energy, and other people tried to make me feel bad about it. I was often conflicted.

This was especially true when it came to my family. I grew up with three brothers, and unfortunately, we didn't have the information about Intangible Drivers when we were young and figuring ourselves out. We were pretty competitive and would use any perceived weakness to tease each other to make ourselves feel good.

In addition to being a "know-it-all," I was also asked to join the "gifted students group" at school. I don't believe I'm any smarter than my brothers. I think the school could identify my intelligence because I pursued learning and was vocal with answers during class.

The biggest thing I remember about the "gifted students group" was that my brothers would make fun of me for it. As I said, it's not that I'm smarter than my brothers; it had more to do with me being very different from all of them. I'm the only Teacher among the four of us, and being in a "smart kid club" just made the difference between my brothers and me seem even more prominent, which led to me having many insecurities, like, "Is there something wrong with me?" I had yet to learn about uniqueness and the fact that everyone views the world, and everything in it, differently. Were my thoughts and motivators that much different from my brothers? YES. But as a boy, it felt like being "different" was wrong.

WHO AM I

I am a Teacher. This means that I want other people to understand not just the *what* but also the *why*. A Teacher will state a fact and might sound like a Perceiver, but they really want to talk about the why. They want you to understand. I find great joy in determining the cause of a circumstance, event, or situation. Finding out the cause of an issue can help people intentionally fix that issue. I love problem-solving.

Teachers are constantly thinking about why things are the way they are, and all they want is to explain it to someone so that others will understand. Commonly, they have multiple ways to explain the same thing, and they will keep explaining from various points of view until they feel as though the other person understands.

CONFIRMATION QUESTIONS

Without trying, do you instantly begin to commentate when a subject is brought up? Do you feel the need to explain the reason why something is the way it is or the reason why something is occurring? Do you get energized when you see the light in someone's eyes showing that they understand?

Do you think you are a Teacher? Who do you know that might be a Teacher?

DIRECTION

Like Perceivers, Teachers are focused on the past because something has had to exist for there to be a reason why. However, Teachers aren't focused infinitely backward like Perceivers. Once they land on a good why, they are done focusing backward.

I have a fourteen-year-old son who is very interested in baseball. Every summer, I find myself wanting to help him understand the game and his ability to play the game better and better during the season. I often find myself only thinking about the games he *has* played and how he can perform better than in the *past*. As good as this can be for him, I also recognize I miss some opportunities to help him prepare for *future* games. My brain just naturally focuses on events that have already occurred. I certainly can use my imagination to think of the future; it's just harder for me. Since I get energy explaining the reason for something, something must have already existed.

When I make a mistake, I can spend enormous amounts of time looping about it in my brain. The story replays repeatedly, and I try to understand more precisely what went wrong. If I don't get help moving forward, I could be prone to depression, thinking that mistakes can never be righted and my behaviors changed moving forward. I appreciate future-focused family and friends that allow me to commentate on my mistakes and then help encourage me to move forward and know I will do better in the future.

My future-focused friends appreciate that I can help them step into the past and figure out what went wrong. Since they naturally run forward, it's harder for them to step back. Many of them have expressed how much they appreciate my ability to break down the past and figure out WHY it went wrong for them. Then I simply get out of their way and let them run forward with their new plan. They naturally know how to move forward. If I don't get out of their way, I might continue to hold them back into their past.

METHOD

I'm definitely a speaking Intangible Driver. I remember being shushed most of my life. I wanted to commentate on everything, so my parents, teachers, and friends always asked me to be quiet and let others participate.

I grew up with friends who were all very interested in hunting, fishing, and hiking in the woods. I remember tagging along with them because they were my friends, even though I never really had a passion for what they were doing. They used to tease me for not knowing all the outdoor techniques. What they didn't realize is that I didn't care about *doing* outdoor activities. My favorite times with them were when we were just hanging out and talking - when we were getting to know each other.

THE WHY EFFECT

I want others to understand why something happens. That's why I enjoyed my math classes so much, because I remember learning the how and why behind the equations that I was trying to solve. When I learned why a problem was solved in a certain way, it helped me solve any other problem like it.

I served in the Marine Corps, and I remember mail-call was one of the greatest events during boot camp. A few times a week, our drill instructors would have us gather in what they called a "school circle" to wait in anticipation for any letters we may have had from home. It seemed strange, but the drill instructors seemed to care more about how we sat down than about the mail. This was common during most of our platoon instructions. We would run to the drill instructor after he yelled, "School-Circle!" We'd run and sit at his feet. Then he'd yell, "Right over left!" This was the strange part, why did they make us sit with our legs like a pretzel? It was especially hard for the bigger recruits, most of whom hadn't sat like this since boyhood. Think about it, when was the last time you saw a grown man sit in this fashion?

As a Teacher, this left me unsettled and frustrated because I knew I couldn't ask why. One of the lessons the drill instructors were teaching the recruits was "Instantaneous Obedience to Orders." I knew the reason for this lesson: do what I tell you to do *immediately* because if this was combat and you wait to follow orders, you (and possibly other Marines) will die! This lesson of "Instantaneous Obedience to Orders" helped me move past not knowing the reason behind most of the orders given to me and my fellow recruits.

Eight weeks into boot camp, we finally got to shoot the rifles we had to carry around for the last two months, and on that very first day at the Rifle Range, I found my reason. One of the four positions required of us to fire our rifles was the sitting position, the very "right over

When I found out that my ID was a Teacher, it made everything make sense.

left" position we've had to sit in daily. The drill instructors knew this was a difficult way to sit for many recruits, but by the time it was Rifle Range week, none of us blinked an eye! There was a benefit, we finally knew why, and I still feel at ease every time I think about this story. Other Intangible Drivers might have just recognized the process and maybe even appreciated it. But for me, as a Teacher, it was a tremendous relief to understand the *why* and to know everyone else now understood the *why*.

When I found out that my ID was a Teacher, it made everything make sense. I was finally settled. I knew there was a purpose to my life! I was able to see that my real friends were the people who wanted me to be *more* of that Teacher that I had discovered!

A friend of mine and I get lunch together every week. Recently he shared with me that when I tell a story or explain something to him, I often finish my sentences saying, "Right?" I was unaware I had been doing this as if it was an unconscious twitch, if you will. However, I also immediately understood that I'm trying to make sure that I'm being heard. When I teach, I want people to hear me, to understand, and if I'm unsure if the person heard me, I will try different methods to confirm that I am heard, including finishing every sentence with the question, "Right?"

To help a Teacher feel settled and valued, tell them you understand. Even repeat back to them what they shared to prove you understand. If you want to make their day, then make a big deal out of understanding. Show them the light in your eyes, give them a smile, and express your understanding through your face, as well as your words.

THE HOW CONNECTION

Teacher HOWs don't just want you to understand; they want to be the ones to give the understanding. They are the ones who will be the first to start commentating on a topic. They are not settled until they do the teaching.

Whenever I interact with other Teacher HOWs, we have a blast. We both get to explain something new, diving down deeper and deeper rabbit trails starting from a single fact, but to the outsider, it probably looks like we're interrupting and talking over each other. Every other sentence is broken up by one of us jumping in saying something like, "That's because…" or, "Actually, the reason that happens is…"

This is where people often struggled with me growing up. As a Teacher HOW, I wanted to be the one to explain something. I love explaining something, and as I've grown up, I've learned when the right time is to explain something because I want people to *want* to hear me. I try to make sure that I'm explaining things for their benefit, and I've had to learn to listen to others the way I'd want them to listen to me because the Teacher HOW part of me wants just to jump in and start explaining, and that can be really frustrating for others.

MISUNDERSTOOD

The times I've felt the most misunderstood have been during extreme emotional arguments, be it with a family member or significant other. My mentality is always to understand, to focus on, and analyze the facts of the disagreement. I can come off as unfeeling, and people have accused me of acting like a robot. What they don't realize, and what I don't show very well, is that I do feel. I feel strongly. I'm a very passionate person. However, my need and desire to solve and understand a problem can often get the best of me.

I can't express enough how much I enjoy explaining facts, to the point that I tend to give some kind of commentary on just about everything that is happening around me. This has caused people to think of me as a know-it-all. They sometimes feel like I'm trying to show off all my knowledge. I get excited explaining the why behind things, which can be misunderstood as me feeling I'm smarter than everyone else. When I was younger and more insecure, this sometimes caused me to shut down and not share my thoughts. I wanted certain people to like me, and I put on a front so that they wouldn't see the real me. I ended up being miserable. I am secure in who I am now and understand the value of my Intangible Driver. I also know that my energy will come from me being my true self, and I appreciate those who want me to be me.

The other way that Teachers are misunderstood is the sheer amount of talking. Because their objective is to help you understand, if you never let them know that you do, they aren't settled. If they don't know that you understand, they feel like they would be doing you a disservice if they didn't *continue* explaining something. The reality is that they simply aren't aware that you understand. As soon as you let them know, they will happily cease and desist *because* they've done their job!

If a Teacher starts explaining something the other person already understands, the other person can begin to tune out the Teacher and feel burdened by the sheer amount of information. If they don't communicate to the Teacher that they understand and just stop listening, the Teacher may see the light in their eyes going darker, and they feel like the other person understands less. Of course, they're going to keep talking! They feel like the person is falling down a hole, and they're the only one with a rope to get them out! All the other person has to do is share that they understand, and the Teacher can feel settled.

UNHEALTHY USE OF ID

I have a passion for helping people. However, I've learned that how I help people is just as important as the actual help I give them. There have been many times when someone I've tried teaching has not actually wanted me to teach them. In a prideful mentality, I would only consider that what that person really needed was for me to convince them that they really needed what I have to offer, and that often led me to the point of yelling. As if what they really needed was for me to scream at them. They'll get it then, right? As important as teaching is to me, I now know that the way and reason I teach is more important than what I'm teaching.

I worked at a popular coffee chain when I was younger. One of the roles I had was Trainer. I could see a growth in my ability to teach over the years of experience I had training new employees. One particular woman who was brought on was highly detailed in how she cleaned our espresso machines. Her standards of cleanliness were much higher than mine and the company's standard, and it caused her to spend too much time on the project. As her trainer, this amount of cleaning was different from what I had taught her. How would I approach her? What was my plan of attack? Just that — "Attack"!

At the time, I was under the impression that the louder and more direct I was, the more likely the person would be to learn what I set out to teach them. I would often yell, thinking it would drive the point deeper. Not only was this a poor way of teaching since the lessons I was teaching were not met with positive emotion, but it was also causing the person to see me as a lousy teacher. The thing I cared about the most and wanted to be the best at had turned into the very thing the people I was training didn't want from me.

I worked with the woman for three years, and it took about two years before our relationship was repaired. Two years of me having to undo the damage I caused. Two years of me having to work hard to turn that negative emotion into a positive. Now I wonder what our working life would have been like if I had those two years to build upon instead of fix?

Unfortunately, the ability to help others understand can cause the Teacher to look at everything one way: they are the teacher. The problem with this is that we often become unwilling to be the student. We can become unteachable and refuse to hear the views and understanding of others. If you're a Teacher, how do you want others to respond to you when you teach? How do you respond to others when they teach you?

Additionally, part of interacting with others means letting them have part of the conversation. When Teachers are in an unhealthy spot, they can have a hard time allowing others to share their perspectives. Teachers might feel that since they know the why they should be the ones to explain it in great detail. This mentality can cause a Teacher to talk for long periods without giving room for someone else to share. Teachers who learn how to give other people space to talk will find that the other person will be more engaged and *want* to listen to them more.

CAREERS

College and university professors are often Teacher HOWs. They get energy from giving a lecture, citing a textbook reference, and preparing materials to reinforce their understanding. K-12 educators tend to be Servers and Compassion IDs and focus more on ensuring a safe environment for children to develop physically, emotionally, and mentally. The Teacher ID generally doesn't focus as much on nurturing the students and therefore are not as attracted to positions in general education.

A Teacher WHY is very commonly a problem-solver and loves looking at puzzles to figure out the solution. They are frequently in other occupations that focus on the why and understanding, such as critics, engineers, and doctors. While law enforcement is mainly made up of Perceivers, detectives are often Teachers because they want to solve a puzzle. Teachers who interact well with people usually excel in technology and executive training fields.

RELATIONSHIPS

Teachers tend to be attracted to other Teachers. They each get to explain something to someone who is passionate about understanding.

Servers can have a hard time with Teachers because a Server is focused on the need. A Server will explain a reason and give understanding so long as that is the need and nothing more. A Teacher will explain as much understanding as possible, even if it isn't necessary. This focus on understanding and commentating regardless of the individual's need tends to bother Servers because they want to adjust to people.

Additionally, a Teacher will blatantly state the reason to pursue truth regardless of how it makes people feel. This can be a hard truth to hear, and the Teacher doesn't have a problem stating it. Servers and Compassions may have a hard time with this, especially if the truth will cause pain.

CHILDREN: PARENTING AND TEACHING

The most important thing to realize about Teacher-WHY is that they are very hard to interact with for long periods if they aren't Teacher-Teacher. When Teacher-WHY isn't also Teacher-HOW, the listener can often feel like they are being tested or having to solve a puzzle because they aren't given the reason!

When a student is described as intelligent and difficult, they will tend to be Teacher-WHY and not Teacher-HOW. Once this is understood, the child can be taught why others are impatient with them. (After all, the Teacher-WHY wants to understand why this is, and believing others are stupid is not a healthy conclusion.)

When it comes to Teacher-HOW, I like to advise children to be a "counter-puncher." What does that mean? I'm glad you asked for an explanation!

In boxing, most people jab to set up their punches. This can be seen as someone initiating a conversation by asking others questions or sharing quick facts about themselves. However, a small minority of boxers wait for the other fighter to initiate their punch because it leaves an opening. These boxers respond to a punch being thrown by countering with their own punch. Likewise, I tell Teacher-HOWs to wait until others teach before they ask if they want to know the reason why.

Children who have a past ID can come off as awkward because they tend to initiate the discussion by going backward, which in the case of Teacher will sound like this, "Did you know that...?" This is why Teachers are seen as "know-it-alls." However, there is another reason why Teachers tend to "know-it-all"...

One of the benefits of being a Teacher is you will tend to be more intelligent. Why? (Again, I'm glad you asked!) It turns out that we, as humans, only learn 25% of information directly. This is why people have to repeat something three times before they fully grasp it. However, it turns out we learn much more effectively when we teach something! Teachers get energy teaching, which makes them able to learn things three times quicker than other people. Notice, this ability isn't confined to Teachers. You can help any child learn three times faster if you allow them to teach! This leads me to my last point...

Give children who are Teachers the opportunity to Teach! Intentionally ask them to explain something to you or a group of people. It can be very frustrating and demotivating to children who are Teachers that are prevented from explaining anything simply because of their age.

SELF HELP

If you are a Teacher, an area that you can grow in that will positively affect your relationships is asking people if they want to know why before you start explaining something. When people feel like it is their choice, they'll be more apt to pay attention to what you're trying to explain, even if they're only saying yes to be polite.

People might say no, but did you want to explain something to someone who was going to try to ignore you?

The key to being a confident Teacher is to realize that one of the values you offer is that constant desire to understand. Still, other people usually only want that understanding when they need it or when it interests them. Having a vast wealth of knowledge is a tremendous value. Once a Teacher learns how to deliver that knowledge for the benefit of others, they'll see people begin to recommend their expertise to others, giving the Teacher a broader and broader audience to teach.

CHEAT SHEET

Teacher-Perceiver
Wants people to be aware of an issue to help people understand why the issue exists. "The sundae wasn't balanced correctly to make it all the way from the counter to our table."

Teacher-Teacher
Wants people to understand why an issue exists to help people understand why that issue exists. "The sundae wasn't balanced correctly on the plate."

Teacher-Compassion
Wants to bear the emotional pain of people to help people understand why an issue exists. "Don't feel bad about the way the sundae wasn't balanced on the plate. It could have happened to anyone."

Teacher-Giver
Wants to give a tangible gift or improvement to help people understand why an issue exists. "Let me buy you a sundae on a bigger plate so it can be balanced."

Teacher-Server
Wants to fill needs to help people understand why an issue exists. "I'm going to tell them they ought to put sundaes on bigger plates."

Teacher-Administrator
Wants to coordinate a group of people to help people understand why an issue exists. "Ted, Marcia...did you see how small the plate was?"

Teacher-Exhorter
Wants to encourage people about the future to help people understand why an issue exists. "Next time, we will eat at the counter, so you won't have to balance the sundae on that small plate."

FAMOUS EXAMPLES OF TEACHER-WHYS

Teacher-Perceiver: Sherlock Holmes (detective), Dwight Shrute (TV show *The Office*)

Teacher-Perceiver is one Intangible Driver combination that can have a lot of difficulties feeling understood. When people do take the time to understand them, they often feel very touched.

Often, without trying, Teacher-Perceivers can make people feel like they're stupid. A perfect example of a Teacher-Perceiver is Sherlock Holmes. He arrives at a crime scene and sees a woman dressed for travel wearing a pink suit, a pink hat, and pink nails, and he shouts, "Pink!"

Everyone looks at him as if he has gone crazy, and no one responds. Sherlock realizes no one understands, even though he feels like he has given them everything they could possibly need to understand, and he asks, "What must it be like in your heads? Is it nice? Is it peaceful?"

Now he's perceiving on everyone else because he feels like no one is even trying to figure out the puzzle with him. If someone responded with, "She's dressed for flying, she must have had a suitcase, and it must also be the same shade of pink!" Then Sherlock would say, "That's what I said." Ideally, someone would respond to Sherlock with, "To the airport because we need to find her suitcase!"

If you spend a lot of time with a Teacher-Perceiver, you can help build that relationship by explaining your understanding of their Intangible Driver. Then try to take your time and figure out the understanding they want you to have and respond with a new what. If it takes a solid minute to do that, that's okay. The Teacher-Perceiver will feel like someone finally cares enough to take the time to think about what they said. If you are a Teacher-Perceiver, the first step to having better relationships is to realize that other people don't think like you and will need a little more help to understand. Take your time because if you rush, you'll actually make everyone feel dumb.

Teacher-Teacher: Spock (TV show *Star Trek*), Kingsfield (*Paperchase*)
Teacher-Compassion: Rick Steeves (travel guide)
Teacher-Giver: Advertising executives, Don Draper (TV Show *Mad Men*)
Teacher-Server: Batman, Tour guides
Teacher-Administrator: Dr. Gregory House (TV show *House*)
Teacher-Exhorter: Personal trainers, Chris Traeger (TV Show *Parks and Recreation*)

CHAPTER 5

COMPASSION

"Don't feel bad; it could have happened to anyone."

(OKAY, it's my turn.) Hi, I'm Jonathan, and my Intangible Driver is Compassion. My friends call me the Compassionator. I like that because it makes me feel like they understand my ID is strong like all the other Superheros.

GROWING UP

When my Uncle Aaron was born, he had a brain clot that resulted in him being mentally challenged. He speaks and thinks like a five-year-old. When I was growing up, he would come and visit our family on

Christmas, and he would ask the same questions and say the same things over and over again, just like a little kid. He would always try so hard to interact with us. He would want to play with us kids, but it was tough for him to keep up at the speed at which we did things.

We had a game where you would match different sized shapes together, and they would make a square. One day I watched my uncle's hands shake as he struggled to find out how the pieces fit together. He must have sat there for hours working on this puzzle until I eventually broke down in tears, weeping as I began to realize my uncle's mental condition fully.

"It's not fair that he's like that!" I cried to my parents. "I want him to be better." There was nothing I could do to make my uncle's pain go away, and it just hurt inside me.

Growing up, some people thought my sensitivity was sweet, and others thought I was weak. I was frequently asked why I took everything so seriously and told to toughen up.

WHO AM I

Compassion IDs want people to be able to live and grow with less pain. Compassion wants to relieve the pain that people feel, whether from an undeserved reason, like my uncle's mental condition or a decision that caused their own pain or stepping into uncomfortable situations and growing.

Compassion is like a sponge, and pain is water. Everywhere I look, I see soaking wet people. I am drawn to these soaking wet people. I want the pain that they carry to go away, even if that means I get drenched.

A Compassionator doesn't want to make you feel something; they want to keep you from feeling bad. They can feel what other people are feeling and want to bear that pain. The most significant pain a Compassion ID can experience is knowing that they caused pain to someone else.

CONFIRMATION QUESTIONS

Without trying, do you instantly know who is feeling the most pain when you walk into a room? Do you seem to have a pain radar? Do you hate confrontation? Does it hurt when I tell you that you're causing me pain?

Do you think you are a Compassionator? Who do you know that might be Compassion?

DIRECTION

Compassion IDs are focused on the past. Because pain needs to be present for a Compassionator to kick in, an event has already happened that caused the pain. The pain occurs from something the person already experienced rather than something that they will experience in the future.

If you have a big presentation coming up next Tuesday and feel nervous, the Compassion person will ask you questions about why you're nervous, what led you to be nervous, and will try to help you not feel so nervous. A future-focused Intangible Driver would be more likely to help you strategize your presentation or get you excited about the future event so that you could do a great job. The Compassion ID wants you not to feel pain, whether you do a good job on the presentation or not.

Along with focusing on others' pain, I also tend to dwell on past pains in my own thoughts.

I often invite my parents to special events that happen in my life. I do want them there, but that's not what's driving me to invite them. What drives the invite is something that happened on my 21st birthday. On the day of my 21st birthday, I went to the store with my parents to purchase some alcohol for my party. While we were driving to the store, I asked them if they would be okay not coming to my party. They seemed slightly deflated but said, "Of course. It's your birthday party."

When I went up to the cash register to buy my very first bottle, my parents said to the cashier, "We will buy it." I was shocked and said, "Why? You're not even going to be there." They kindly told me, "Jonathan, if we can't be there, we want to invest in your birthday. This is a way that we can still be a part of it."

To this day, I still feel bad about excluding them. I blocked my parents from a milestone in my life, and I can recall that memory and pain like it was yesterday.

METHOD

While Perceivers and Teachers operate in their Intangible Driver by speaking, Compassion is the first of the IDs that operate by *doing* something. They bear your pain by feeling what you feel.

Compassion is something that I show other people. I show them that I care. My Grandfather was a Marine. On a summer vacation with my family when I was about eight years old, my Grandfather started to tell me old war stories. I don't remember any of them, but what I do remember is my mom explaining to me that she had never heard him share as he did with me. She affirmed me for listening to his stories. She explained that I listened to my Grandfather for hours, and he just kept sharing more and more. It wasn't until years later that I realized he felt compassion from me. Compassion people are amazing story hearers! He was telling stories that were painful memories, but because I was bearing that pain, he could feel as if someone was carrying that load with him while he shared and because it didn't feel as overwhelming, he kept sharing!

My favorite example of a Compassion ID is Spider-Man. If you've read the comics or watched the cartoons, Spider-Man reveals that he never uses his full strength when fighting bad guys because he doesn't want to hurt anyone too badly.

Instead, he starts every confrontation by trying to talk the person out of their bad behavior and then cracks jokes while he webs people up with as little violence as possible. After he gets the bad guys tied up, he'll even leave a note for the police to help them take care of it!

Remember the Spidey Sense? Spider-Man can sense danger before it happens to him or the people around him. He's sensing the pain that's coming! Compassions have a similar ability; super-empathy. Compassions sense the pain around them and can feel their way through a challenging interaction with people who have a lot of trauma. Some people call this an "Empath."

THE WHY EFFECT

I want other people not to feel bad. They could feel better emotionally, physically, spiritually, or mentally. I want to take a human who is dead and be a "defibrillator" to them. I want to shock their heart with the electricity of my being for them to be alive again. Once they are alive, I want to move on to the next person. Once they are awake, I want them to look at me and say, "Thank you, Jonathan. I feel so much better." and then hug me and go on their way.

A friend of mine asked me if I was willing to come to the hospital with him. My friend's brother had an accident at the mill where he was working. A machine broke, and a part of it flew out, hit a huge metal table, and slammed into him, absolutely shattering his pelvis.

When we saw his brother in the hospital, he was in rough shape, but he was on a lot of medication to manage the pain. He said the painkillers were working pretty well, but he complained about how much his tailbone hurt because of the bed. I asked what would help. He said the nurse suggested getting a small inner tube to put under his backside. Wanting him to not be in pain no matter the cost, I looked at my friend and gave him the expression that we had to get the inner tube.

We went to a pharmacy, and thankfully they knew exactly what we wanted. We went back to the hospital, and my friend handed the inner tube to his nurse, the nurse slid the inner tube under his brother, and his brother's eyes got wide as he exclaimed, "Oh my gosh! That feels so much better." I started giggling uncontrollably! I was so happy!

THE HOW CONNECTION

Compassion is one Intangible Driver that looks very different in the WHY and HOW positions. A Compassion WHY with a non-compassion HOW always has something they can intentionally do or say, like perceiving as a Compassion-Perceiver, or serving as a Compassion-Server, while they're trying to find out what a person feels. They just focus on their HOW ID until they know what the other person is feeling.

Compassion-Servers tend to be the kindest, smoothest people in the world. They'll focus on filling your needs, being fully attentive to you until they find out how you feel. Then they'll try to help you not feel bad. They can be a little awkward until they find out what you feel, but it's minor.

Compassion in the HOW position is very different. They will try to accomplish something, such as making you aware as a Perceiver-Compassion or helping you feel excited as an Exhorter-Compassion, but they do it by first feeling what you feel. Until they know how you feel, they have an intense struggle with how to interact with you. They can come across as highly awkward until they know what a person is feeling. When people finally share, they suddenly turn smooth and charming and can help the person incredibly well.

A great example of the difference between a Compassion HOW and a Compassion WHY is looking at a Compassion-Perceiver versus a Perceiver-Compassion.

In the movie *Almost Famous*, the lead character William, is a Compassion-Perceiver. He spends the entire film trying to relieve people's pain by pointing things out and showing that he cares. This causes most of the other people in the movie to take advantage of him.

Contrastively, George Costanza from Seinfeld is a Perceiver-Compassion. George spends every season alternating between being terrified of causing pain and emptying his pain out on the people around him, and he struggles with being incredibly awkward. A challenge with being a Compassion HOW is it takes balancing the caring and the awkward, and when it's done right, it can be amazing!

HOW TO HELP

Years ago, a friend of mine noticed that I would hold everything in until one final event would happen, and I would blow up and lash out at others. Of course, to this last person, it appeared I was blowing up over the slightest issue seemingly out of nowhere. This would cause me to feel horrible and hold in my frustrations longer until I would blow up even bigger. This cycle kept continuing. My friend said to me, "Jonathan, why don't you call me and get your pain out before you blow up at others. You can even blow up at me." I realized that Compassion IDs have a pain meter, and when that pain meter gets too full, it has to be relieved to continue to bear the pain of others, and unfortunately, sometimes the way it gets relieved is by blowing up.

Many people who go to prison are Compassion IDs who never let their pain out until it was too much and too late, and they lost control in a very explosive way.

The worst part is as soon as that moment is over, if the Compassion person doesn't realize that they need to share that pain in a healthy way, they just refill their pain meter by feeling all of the pain they just caused to someone else. It's a terrible cycle.

What reached me is that my friend said I am not an effective leader when I am full of pain. When I am full of pain, he explained that I am too focused on myself and not focused on other people's feelings. He motivated me to safely remove my pain by saying how my pain can hurt other people if I don't deal with it the right way.

Another key to helping Compassion IDs is to realize they will actively try to feel what you feel, and until they know what you are feeling, they can appear very awkward. Compassion is one of the most awkward Intangible Drivers until they know how you are feeling. Once they know what you are feeling, they know exactly how to interact with you, and they'll become the sweetest, most caring friend. The key to helping someone who is Compassion is to share what is bothering you and let them help you feel better!

MISUNDERSTOOD

On multiple occasions, I have heard someone say, "If you want someone to cry with you, talk to Jonathan." However, I am not going to cry just because someone else is crying. I am not going to laugh just because someone is laughing. Feeling what someone is feeling doesn't mean that you only mirror their emotion. Someone could tell me a story about something amazing that happened, they could cry tears of joy, and I could laugh out of joy, as we are connecting over the emotion of joy, not simply the expression of it. When people are crying, I don't connect with them until I know why they are crying. I need to know where the pain is coming from to feel connected to the emotion that they are showing. I need to know someone's reason or story for them crying.

Another common misunderstanding is Compassion IDs are often considered emotional and weak because they feel the pain of others, especially in a culture that values the typical masculine stereotypes. This leads to Compassion IDs often being bullied.

The truth is Compassion IDs are the strongest Intangible Driver. It takes a strong person to bear the pain of others and to help carry that pain while assisting the person in growing through their difficult situation.

UNHEALTHY USE OF ID

Years ago, I heard about a man who had caused a lot of pain to some friends of mine. I heard that there was a close group of guys who were hanging out, and this man started coming around and broke up their friendship. I was upset. I would say to my friends, "It's so unfair that all of that happened to you!"

One of those friends told me to stay away from that man, so I never found out the whole story. I didn't probe to find out all of the facts until years later. I enabled my friends by only listening to their feelings instead of looking for the facts as well.

Years later, when none of those friends connected with me anymore, I found out all the facts of that story. It turns out that man had been trying to help those guys, but they had turned around and gossiped about him instead. I don't talk to any of those old friends anymore, but I've become close with that man, and I've realized that enabling my friends all those years ago prevented me from having a great friendship with this man.

> **COMPASSION IS THE STRONGEST INTANGIBLE DRIVER, BUT OUR SOCIETY DOESN'T VALUE IT BECAUSE IT SEES EMOTIONS AS WEAK.**

Enabling others is a common misuse for Compassion IDs when they are in an unhealthy place mentally and emotionally. Enabling is when a person tries to relieve pain in one step.

I have another friend who was married to a chronic, enabling wife. He told her he had to write an uncomfortable email to his boss, giving him bad news. A healthy Compassion ID would have been able to help my friend get his feelings out, figure out his first step, and support him stepping into and through the challenging situation. Instead, she told him not to worry, to sit down and eat dinner, and she wrote the email for him. The result was that my friend was less and less able to handle stress at work until he would spend sleepless nights worrying about the outcome of a single sentence from a conversation he had with his boss. Enabling doesn't help strengthen people or relieve their pain in the long term. It actually causes them to become weaker.

Another way Compassion IDs can misuse their uniqueness is when they fall into weakness. Compassion is the strongest Intangible Driver, but our society doesn't value it because it sees emotions as weak. When a Compassion ID starts to believe this lie, they begin to think they aren't strong enough to handle pain. Because they feel the pain, they think something is wrong with them.

When a Compassion ID gets into weakness, they tend to become apathetic, refusing to handle anything challenging or difficult. They end up avoiding confrontation because it can cause pain in the short term. In order to get out of weakness, the Compassion person needs to step into something outside of themselves that is for the benefit of other people. That will help get the focus off of their own feeling, which is draining for the Compassion person.

RELATIONSHIPS

Exhorters and Compassion IDs tend to get along very well for a while. Exhorters want others to feel what they feel and often start conversations by sharing their emotions. Compassions feel awkward until they know what someone feels, so they love that Exhorters are willing to share upfront.

As time goes on, the Exhorter feels more and more that they can just share all of their own feelings without worrying about what anyone else feels. Eventually, they can start to neglect the Compassion person's needs, resulting in the Compassion person feeling taken for granted.

If the Exhorter learns how to take a step back and focus on the Compassion person, the two will grow an extremely close bond. I know a few power couples who have this dynamic!

Compassion people tend to be attracted to Perceivers. The Perceiver is trying to make people aware of the problem, and people tend to feel pain, which is when the Compassion person feels pulled into the situation. It is the perfect opportunity to bear the pain to help others grow!

As mentioned before, Compassion and Servers get along very well. Compassion wants to relieve pain, and Servers want to fill needs, and these two traits often overlap. Servers have a hard time saying no. This tends to cause them to be overworked with packed schedules, which means a lot of stress and pain. Compassion people love to help relieve that pain for the Server.

Compassion can have a hard time with Administrators because the Compassion is so focused on the individual, while Administrators see the individual in terms of the group. The Administrator isn't a cold, uncaring person, but they can come off like they don't care about the individual's need or the pain of a person. Compassion can get frustrated with Administrators and might feel like the Administrator is cold and uncaring or that the Administrator is manipulating the people around them.

CAREER OPTIONS

Common job fields for Compassion IDs might be nursing, education, counseling, and spiritual leadership. Research has shown that less than 5% of public school teachers have a Teacher ID.

Educators must set up an ideal learning environment where students feel safe, calm, and have room to learn and grow. Compassion IDs want to relieve the pain that comes with growth, and in school, there often is a lot of growth and a lot of pain. A school teacher can be in contact daily with dozens of students who might be in pain. That's dozens of opportunities each day to practice Compassion.

Counselors and spiritual leaders spend a lot of time helping relieve people of specific pain one on one. A pastor might spend three hours a week giving a sermon, but the rest of the week, they might be holding office hours to help their members with any personal struggle.

Many nurses will tell you that they are the ones who actually spend time with the patient and *really* know what's going on with each of them. Nurses are often Compassion because healing takes time and involves going through pain. Part of a nurse's job is caring for the patients while the doctor diagnoses and applies a treatment.

CHILDREN: PARENTING AND TEACHING

During middle school, Compassion IDs often go through trauma because they feel other people's pain during what is usually one of the most stressful times of one's life. A Compassion kid is in class, and the whole class gets reprimanded harshly. The kids feel embarrassed, and it's a seven out of ten on the pain scale. The Compassion instantly feels the pain from their classmates and then feels their own pain, another seven out of ten. The Compassion is now feeling their own pain and the other kids' pain, and it becomes a fourteen out of ten. Anything over ten is beyond what someone can hold back, and the Compassion kid starts to tear up. The other kids see them and say, "Wow, you must be a *baby* since that's all it took to make you cry!"

At first, the Compassion feels like the rest of the kids are unfeeling robots. As time goes on, the Compassion sees that more people think it's weird to feel all of that pain. They start to believe that they are weak, that they are the weird ones, and they begin to hold things in. Notice, this is especially difficult for boys, and any authority figure telling them not to cry because it shows weakness is only making the issue worse.

A mom asked me to speak to her Compassion son. A lunch monitor had called him a baby when he had teared up during an incident at the lunch table. I told him Compassion needs to learn that they are stronger than those other kids. Those other kids couldn't even feel anything beyond a ten out of ten because that's the most you can feel on your own. Compassion can feel twenty out of ten and bear it. That's true strength. His learning how to embrace and direct this superpower has led to him communicating it to his friends so he can help them.

SELF HELP

One of the most critical lessons a Compassion person needs to learn is how to confront others. Confrontation is tense! Compassions often feel that they are going to cause pain by confronting, which often leads them to enable others' destructive behaviors. While in reality, Compassions are the one Intangible Driver that can confront people without causing pain.

When a Compassion confronts, the other person is likely to hear them out because they feel the empathy and care that Compassion gives off. When a Compassion wants to help someone get on the superhighway of growth, I always encourage them to channel a little Perceiver to help people see what they need to change, and then they can bear their pain as they work on that issue.

Compassion IDs can sometimes be easy to manipulate because they are attracted to pain and often hate confrontation. When Compassions see others arguing, they tend to side with the person in the most pain, even if that person is being abusive.

If someone shares a story about their pain, but they don't have a resolution, Compassions tend to be attracted to them. Often, we have had to help Compassion ID women attracted to destructive guys because of their compassion. They see a guy who has excessive behavioral problems, like drug addiction or abuse, and they see a lot of pain to relieve, which puts them right into their ID and gives them energy.

While those situations where a person has an addiction or is abusive are genuinely in need of compassion, they become easy to fake out or manipulate. I knew a Compassion man with two teenage children that would get in fights while he was at work. It would get so bad that his daughter would call him at work, and as soon as she started talking about the problem, she would begin to cry. Often, the man would then side with his daughter because it seemed that she was in pain.

Unfortunately, the daughter was manipulating her Compassion father. She had learned through experience that if she cried, her father would melt and enable her. It would be beneficial for Compassion IDs to understand better and identify when others are trying to take advantage of their incredible uniqueness.

> **People who have destructive behaviors often fake pain to attract Compassion IDs.**

Men will even fake pain to get Compassion women to sleep with them, and women will fake pain to get Compassion men to give them more attention. People who have destructive behaviors often fake pain to attract Compassion IDs because they will always need someone to come to their aid when they get into trouble because of their bad behaviors and habits. They will become chronic complainers, whining and complaining about how difficult life is to get Compassion IDs on their side. They struggle to get anyone else on their side because the other IDs will try to focus them on resolving their problems. They often can manipulate Compassion and avoid responsibility.

The key for Compassion IDs is to find someone who is *not* Compassion that they can trust and share their own pain. Compassion is one of the IDs that doesn't naturally like being on the receiving end of compassion. Perceivers struggle with being perceived on. Teachers struggle to be taught. Compassions struggle to receive compassion because they feel like they're going to cause pain.

Think of it this way; Compassion naturally feels the pain of others. They cannot turn it off, *and* they believe the worst thing they could do is cause someone else to feel pain. They don't realize that some people do not feel other people's pain automatically. A Compassion person needs to learn that they can share their pain with someone who isn't Compassion to get it out and that this will not cause that person pain.

If you're Compassion, do you want to live your life holding back your pain until it comes out with you hurting others? Would you rather find someone who can hear your pain without it hurting them?

CHEAT SHEET

Compassion-Perceiver
Wants to make people aware of an issue to bear the emotional pain of others. "It's just a sundae."

Compassion-Teacher
Wants to help people understand why an issue exists to bear the emotional pain of others. "It wasn't your fault. They didn't put the sundae on a big enough plate."

Remember, Compassion people tend to avoid confrontation, as they are worried that they will cause pain by pointing out someone's flaws. However, Compassion is the one Intangible Driver that can actually deliver bad news *without* causing pain. They just don't realize it. In the television show House M.D., House's best friend is Dr. Wilson, a Compassion-Teacher. As an oncologist, a significant part of his job is informing patients they have cancer, often telling them that they will die. When he tells people they have cancer, because of his incredible Compassion, they end up grateful to him for telling them, even thanking him.

Compassion-Compassion
Wants to bear the emotional pain of people to bear the emotional pain of others. "Don't feel bad. It could have happened to anyone."

Compassion-Giver
Wants to give a tangible gift or improvement to people to bear the emotional pain of others. "Let me buy you another sundae so you won't feel bad."

Compassion-Server
Wants to fill a need to bear the emotional pain of others. "I'll clean this up. It's no big deal."

Compassion-Administrator
Wants to coordinate a group of people to bear the emotional pain of others. "Ted, do you remember when Marcia dropped her sundae?"

Compassion-Exhorter
Wants to encourage people about the future to bear the emotional pain of others. "Next time we come here, you'll be laughing about this."

FAMOUS EXAMPLES OF COMPASSION-WHYS

Compassion-Perceiver: Obi-wan (*Star Wars*), Steve Wozniak (Co-Founder of Apple), Roger Waters (musician), Jackson Browne (musician)

Compassion-Teacher: Colossus, C3PO (*Star Wars*), Scotty Smalls (*The Sandlot*), Walter White (TV show *Breaking Bad*), Bruce Banner (aka The Hulk)
Compassion-Compassion: A Martyr, Sidney Carton (book *A Tale of Two Cities*)
Compassion-Giver: Jason Bourne (*Bourne Identity*)
Compassion-Server: Anakin Skywalker (*Star Wars*), Jimmy Fallon (actor/comedian), Spiderman
Compassion-Administrator: Big Brothers-Big Sisters
Compassion-Exhorter: Ron Weasley (book/movie *Harry Potter*), Stan Lee (actor/director)

CHAPTER 6

GIVER

"Let me buy you another sundae."

IN THIS chapter, we're going to hear from my Giver friend, Junko.

Junko works as an administrator in the education field. She has had a huge part in getting the Intangible Drivers adopted by teachers and administrators in the field, all because she saw how much better this could make the classroom environment. Once the educators learn their ID and the ID of their students, they reach out to us to let us know all of the most challenging students they'd been dealing with are suddenly easy cases. Junko loves to make the classroom environment better by giving teachers this valuable information.

Junko is always giving. Most of my friends have a t-shirt or koozie relating to their ID that was custom made by her.

Junko is one of the most generous, level-headed people I know, and she channels her Giver excellently. I'm excited for her to give you all the details on how her Giver ID works!

Junko, will you allow everyone the opportunity to hear your story?

GROWING UP

Hi all, my name is Junko, and I'm a Giver.

As a child, I always enjoyed giving homemade gifts to family and friends. I would spend hours making personalized cards and crafts to give to others just to see the smile on their faces when they received them. I felt that by giving them something personalized, they would appreciate it more and have a better day. Despite my mother's strong objections, I also gave away my flute, Barbies, and all of the homemade Barbie clothes (that my mother made) to cousins that I felt needed them more than I did.

I also gave just about any friend or family member a hug freely without it feeling awkward to anyone. I didn't understand why hugging someone could be so uncomfortable for my brother, but he is not a Giver!

As a teenager, my friends would often come to me for advice on making things better or handling problems that they had with other friends. I was often seen as the problem-solver or peacekeeper in my group of friends.

However, I would also become frustrated when people didn't show appreciation when I offered my help. If that happened, I would shut down or refuse to help them further, which often resulted in people asking me what was wrong. Some people even said that I would hold things over their heads by not sharing what was wrong with me when they shared what was wrong with them.

Once I learned about my Giver Intangible Driver, I realized that I wasn't a bad person! I wasn't intentionally holding things over other people's heads. I was focused on other people. I hated to talk about myself and just wanted to make things better for everyone else.

WHO AM I

Giver IDs want you to receive a tangible gift, such as buying a new ice cream cone. If there is no tangible need, then Givers focus on improving something already good.

They tend to initiate interactions when everything is fine. They want to give you something more or try to make something better.

Giving a tangible gift, affection towards another, advice, or suggestions came naturally to me. This is not natural to others.

Our culture has taught us that when someone offers to give you something or pay for something, the polite thing to do is say "No, thank you," or "That's ok, I got this." But that actually causes pain to a Giver because they feel energized and valued when they get to give. So what's the easiest first step to help a Giver? Let them give!

CONFIRMATION QUESTIONS

Do you get energy when giving to others? Do you get upset or angry when you try to give, and someone won't accept it? Do you like improving things that are already good?

Do you think you are a Giver? Who do you know that might be a Giver?

DIRECTION

Givers are the only ID that are naturally focused on the present moment. They can think fast on their feet and can help others in an emergency. Givers live in the moment. They do not feel comfortable imagining or thinking about the future and do not dwell on the past.

Givers can sometimes be challenging to interact with because they are so focused on the present moment. A Giver will give a gift and move on. They won't dwell on it. They aren't thinking too far forward. They aren't thinking too far backward. This results in other IDs feeling like they cannot connect with the Giver, often resulting in the other IDs determining the Giver is unemotional. My friends often tell me that I have a fantastic poker face because they can't read me.

If a Giver feels bad in a moment, they tend to just move on to the next moment. They don't share their pain. Many Givers do this for years and wind up holding the longest grudges. It could be two decades later before a Giver finally thinks back to the thing that initially frustrated them. I had noticed that my mother, also a Giver, always held the longest grudges, and I never understood why until I learned this information.

METHOD

Givers like to supply something tangible, so we are a *DOing* ID. I have several family members that are Giver HOWs. In the past, my husband would always get frustrated with my mother, a Compassion-Giver, when she insisted on paying for our family when we went out to dinner. He would often say to me, "We are adults with good-paying jobs and can afford to pay for our own meals. Why does she always insist on paying for us?" Before I learned this information, I would just tell him to thank her so that she wouldn't get mad. This information has helped both of us understand that she gets energy and feels valued when she pays for dinner (Giver) so that she could bear our burden and help us grow (Compassion).

THE WHY EFFECT

Giver WHYs focus on what tangible item is needed or how something could be improved. They want others to receive the benefit of the tangible item or improvement.

I want to help make things better, and I feel settled when someone accepts the value that I can offer. For example, I enjoy finding solutions to make a process or procedure better at work, my friends asking me for my advice on a situation, or celebrating events by giving a thoughtful gift.

Givers are focused on other people and do not like any attention to be on themselves, and they do not like to share about themselves. They can appear to be stoic and unemotional.

When I was in college, I thought that I wanted to be an actuary since I was great at math. But I quickly realized that working with numbers was not what I wanted to do because I would not have an opportunity to interact with people. Being a Giver is all about helping or giving to others.

I eventually found the right job for me as a special education coordinator. In that job, I was able to work with students and staff to problem-solve, collaborate and educate children. I got to advise teachers, make plans to help students improve their behaviors, and be part of teams that worked towards improving district policies. As long as I can work with people who want to grow, learn, or make things better, I get energized, and my day flies by.

THE HOW CONNECTION

A Giver HOW is focused on giving a tangible gift. They are not settled until they are acknowledged for their gift and will sometimes become angry if someone does not say "Thank you."

Giver HOWs tend to look generous because they are physically giving things away. A Compassion-Giver will supply a tangible need in the hopes of relieving pain. This person would buy you a new sundae so that you feel better. We tend to see these folks as kind and generous people. On the other hand, a Giver-Compassion will appear both very kind and somewhat unemotional because they are very nice upfront but ultimately focused on getting you what you need. As soon as you get it, they're done.

A Perceiver-Giver will supply a tangible need so that the person is aware of an issue or situation. A friend of mine was moving into an apartment and needed some kitchen supplies. Her grandmother, a Perceiver-Giver, invited my friend over to her house and began pulling out all kinds of pots and pans and other kitchen essentials. She told her granddaughter that she could have all of it. Her granddaughter thanked her Perceiver-Giver grandmother. The next day at a family gathering, the grandmother told other family members and granddaughter how she gave her all of these kitchen items, so now she didn't have to buy them. She wanted to make everyone aware that her granddaughter no longer had to buy all of the new items because she gave them to her.

David, a Giver HOW, was once offered a free book. Just a simple little thing, right? He asked the person how much the book cost, and he was told it was free. He clarified, asking how much the book would cost if it were being sold. The person told him it sells for $15.

David took out a twenty-dollar bill and tried to hand it to the other person. They refused, saying it was supposed to be a free book. David insisted and began to get upset. The person finally accepted the money and said, "Thank you."

David smiled and said, "No, thank *you*." He was happier to have a chance to give someone $20 than if he were to get a free book!

HOW TO HELP

Let us give. A Giver will see some need and want to give something to help take care of it, and when people refuse the offer, we feel disconnected and discouraged. It's so frustrating!

When we offer advice to help make something better, we aren't trying to say that something is wrong or bad. We just naturally see how something can be even better. We will feel awesome if your first response is just a positive word to let us know you have received our gift.

If you feel insecure about our suggestion and respond negatively, we will feel deflated. If you say no or shoot down a suggestion that we make, we will shut down and not want to participate.

Let us give, and just say thank you. It's that simple!

MISUNDERSTOOD

Givers are often misunderstood as unemotional and overly calm or rich and wealthy. While no one has ever thought of me as rich, people often think that I am unemotional or "Super Chill," as if nothing bothers me.

One of the things that upsets me the most is when someone tells me that they think I don't care about anything. I can think of several times in my life that this statement has made me angry and often resulted in an argument.

Most recently, my husband and I were in the process of purchasing some hunting land. This was a very slow process, and things were not moving fast enough for my husband. One day after work, he had asked me if I had heard from the bank on some documents that I had shared with them to process for the closing. When I told him that I hadn't heard from them and hadn't followed up yet, he said to me, "You just don't care!" I was so mad at him for telling me that I don't care. Because I wasn't outwardly stressed out or running around in crisis mode, he felt that I didn't care.

Givers sometimes feel angry that others don't acknowledge or connect with them. Once they learn to share about themselves, what they are thinking and feeling, it will relieve this issue. Often when others struggle to connect with a Giver, it's because the Giver has avoided sharing anything that can connect with others! If the Giver starts sharing, then others will start connecting!

UNHEALTHY USE OF ID

When a Giver tries to give to someone, and it's not accepted, it can cause them to feel upset and misunderstood. This frustration can feel like they were taken from because they were prevented from the opportunity to give. If that pain is bad enough, a Giver may try to relieve their own pain, and they start by taking from others. This is a misuse of their ID. They focus on what they can get rather than what they can give to others.

My friend Mary told me about her first Christmas with her Giver husband. He gave her a fishing pole. She was confused because she never mentioned wanting to fish. He was very excited, and she eventually realized he bought it for himself.

Once they both learned his Giver ID, they were able to keep an eye out for when he wandered off course and started taking rather than giving. He recognized that he struggled with sharing what he wanted. So, he would convince himself of how he could give what he really wanted to someone else disguised as a gift, which would be perceived as a good deed. This is getting rather than giving or simply taking from someone else.

> **SOMETIMES GIVERS WHO HAVE GONE THROUGH TRAUMA CAN FEEL LIKE THEY DON'T HAVE ENOUGH TO GIVE.**

Don Felder, a band member of the Eagles, was known for always making little demo tracks. He would make cassette tapes and give them to the other members of the band. All he wanted to do was give. One of these tapes ended up having the main guitar riff that turned into *Hotel California*, the band's biggest hit, and he wasn't given writing credit for it. When the band got back together to record their next album, Don Felder, who had held a grudge, was ready to get something back from the band. He said he wanted to sing lead on three of the songs for the next album, deciding that it was time to get his due because he didn't feel appreciated. Instead, the band leaders let him record and then took him to dinner while someone else recorded the song that ended up on the album.

Another unhealthy use is sometimes Givers who have gone through trauma can feel like they don't have enough to give and begin collecting things. They'll be afraid to throw things away or get rid of something because someone might need it in the future, and they'll be unable to give. This is how people commonly become hoarders. They believe the solution to their trauma is never to have a situation where they can't give something, so they make sure never to throw anything away.

I have a friend whose grandparents are both Givers, and every Sunday, they would go on a shopping trip to a warehouse retail store. They would buy the items that they needed, plus purchase six to eight extra of each item so that they could give it away to their kids and grandkids and have one or two to spare in case they found out someone else needed it too. This led to them having multiple rooms in their house that were full of stuff! When it came time to help the grandparents move out of their home, the kids found all kinds of never-opened goods.

RELATIONSHIPS

If a Giver wants to have healthy relationships, they need to learn to share their feelings. How would a Giver do that when they hate thinking about themselves? They would realize that there are people in their lives that care about them. To those people, hearing the Giver's thoughts and emotions is a *gift*, especially if those people are Compassion! Once a Giver realizes this, they could start looking for the Compassion IDs in their life and start giving to them.

Givers tend to be attracted to Compassion and Server IDs. In fact, many Compassion IDs test out as Giver because they believe buying someone a sundae will help the person not feel bad. Only when they are forced to choose between buying a sundae or the person not feeling bad, do we find out they are a Compassion.

Compassion, Server, and Giver are in the middle of the spectrum of Intangible Drivers. They are pretty balanced between past and future and are generally focused on other people but struggle to help themselves. Our culture considers these the "Good People" whenever they appear in stories, but of course, we are now starting to see each Intangible Driver's value.

An interesting distinction is between a Giver and a Server. We will look more closely at Servers in the next chapter, but let's examine the difference between them right now to help us understand Givers more.

Both want to fill what they believe is a need. The Giver sees a need as something that can be improved by either giving a tangible gift or providing an idea or solution to make something better. A Server considers a need to be something missing or needs to be fixed.

Imagine two people are working on two different machines. The first person is working calmly, and everything is going well. The second person is swearing and cursing at the machine because it keeps bending the part they're trying to make. The Giver will naturally be drawn to the first person because they want to improve something, and the Server will naturally be drawn to the second to fix the problem.

If the Giver *had* to interact with the person who was having a hard time, they would try to solve the problem by giving something tangible, such as a radio, to call maintenance when issues arise in the future.

If the Compassion or Server had to interact with the person doing well, they would appear awkward because they wouldn't be sure how to interact with them. The Compassion ID would be looking for the pain to relieve, and the Server would be looking for a need to fill, and until they found it, they would struggle with knowing what to say or do. This is where a Perceiver or Teacher could be a great help!

Givers tend to avoid Exhorters and Perceivers because of the extreme focus on the far past or the far future. It can be challenging for them to move that far from the present. Additionally, Exhorters feel a *lot* of emotion, which can make a Giver feel uncomfortable.

CHILDREN: PARENTING AND TEACHING

Giver children tend to be the most confounding ones to raise because they act completely opposite of how parents think, which means their approach needs to be the opposite. For example, rather than

> **THE MOST CHALLENGING ASPECT FOR YOUNG GIVERS IS TO REALIZE THEY ARE DEALING WITH INSECURE PEERS.**

motivating them by telling them to do things for themselves, they need to be motivated by doing things for others.

Elizabeth would always frustrate her parents on the first day of school. They would buy her all the school supplies she needed: a year's worth of pencils, erasers, pens, markers, and even a few rulers. When she came home at the end of the first day, she didn't have any of it left.

Whenever another kid needed something, she would just give them one of her supplies. She'd supply half the class with her pencils, pens, and markers.

Our friend Jonathan Fries, a Compassion-Server, was coaching in a high school with three other coaches, and they split the kids between them, three or four to a coach.

All Jonathan wants to do is serve you to relieve your pain. His group of students had two Giver-Servers and a Server-Server. Givers and Servers can be quickly drained talking about themselves, which was the objective of this meeting. So, Jonathan was trying to get the students to talk about themselves, and they were utterly resisting. Their heads were hanging down, and they weren't saying a word. All of them were extremely drained.

They finish their session, and the coaches all get together to talk about how it went. One of the other coaches, an Administrator, had almost every Intangible Driver represented in his group, which was a dream come true for him. The rest of the coaches had similarly ideal situations. As they all shared about how well it went, Jonathan became upset and said, "We just sat there staring at each other! They didn't share anything! That was my nightmare!"

The next time everyone met, Jonathan realized he needed to share about himself first and turn everything he was doing into an opportunity for the Giver-Servers and the Server-Server to be about someone else's benefit. Once he did that, the students were instantly energized and engaged, and they spent the rest of the sessions having a great time.

The most challenging aspect for young Givers is to realize they are dealing with insecure peers. Remember, a Giver doesn't want to hear a negative response immediately after they offer their gift, especially if it is an idea. However, to insecure people, this gift of improving something can feel like the Giver is saying they are wrong or lacking, which causes them to respond in a defensive or even offensive manner immediately. To the Giver, it feels like the person took the gift and threw it on the ground.

Young Givers need to learn they are looking for a non-negative response, and their feeling in response to the insecurity of others doesn't mean the Giver is a bad person. One way to help the young Giver is to have them begin their response by saying, "I think that's good, and I only say this because I want to help make it better..." before sharing their ideas for improvement.

CAREERS

Givers tend to want to be surrounded by other IDs in the middle of the spectrum like Compassion and Server and might be drawn to industries like manufacturing and education.

A Giver is also likely to work in positions where they can give things away, such as Doctors Without Borders or a philanthropy division of a large corporation. Givers also excel in consulting roles where they help successful businesses improve processes and outcomes.

However, the reality is a Giver can end up in any profession because every profession can be improved!

SELF HELP

When I wanted to grow more in my relationships, I learned how to share my thoughts and feelings with my friends. I learned that my sharing was a value that I could always give them, and it was something that could make our friendship better. I want to give. I want to make things better, so why wouldn't I share with people who want to hear me?

The trick was learning to focus on sharing for *them* instead of for myself.

In the same way that I want to give to others, the people who care about me feel great when they get to give to me. If someone asked me for help and let me give to them, I would feel like they were giving me a benefit. Why would I think the people who care about me feel any differently?

It is so hard for a Giver to ask for help. It feels like I'm acting in opposition to who I am at a fundamental level, but when I started to look at it this way, where asking for help was giving my friends the same opportunity to give that I loved, it became easier to ask for help.

As a Giver, I had to find some way to get over the issue of asking for help because I know I'm not perfect, and if I don't get help growing, then I will eventually be unable to give the way I want. I don't want to end up in the spot where I can't help others because I can't help myself first.

CHEAT SHEET

Giver-Perceiver
Wants to make people aware of an issue in order to give a tangible gift or improvement. "You need another sundae."

Giver-Teacher
Wants to help people understand why an issue exists in order to give a tangible gift or improvement. "I'm going to buy you a sundae on a bigger plate."

Giver-Compassion
Wants to bear the emotional pain of people in order to give a tangible gift or improvement. "Would you feel better if I bought you another sundae?"

Giver-Giver
Wants to give a tangible benefit to people in order to give a tangible gift or improvement. "Let me buy you another sundae."

Giver-Server
Wants to fill an intangible need in order to give a tangible gift or improvement. "Let me clean this up so we can buy you another sundae."

Remember the example with the two people working at two different machines? If the person is Giver-Server, they would want to walk up to *both* people. Giver-Server can get involved in everyone's business because everyone either has a need or is doing well. It's essential for these people to recognize the reason why they are approaching the person. If the person acts like a Giver when the person has a need, it will cause the person in need to get more upset. If the person acts as a Server when the person is doing fine, it will cause the person to become confused.

Giver-Administrator
Wants to coordinate a group of people in order to give a tangible gift or improvement. "Ted, Marcia, let's buy another sundae."

Giver-Exhorter
Wants to encourage people about the future in order to give a tangible gift or improvement. "I'm going to buy you a bigger sundae."

FAMOUS EXAMPLES OF GIVER-WHYS

Giver-Perceiver: Neil Young (musician)
Giver-Teacher: Corporate trainers
Giver-Compassion: Mother Teresa, Charity workers/volunteers
Giver-Giver: Thurston Howell III (TV show *Gilligan's Island*), Philanthropist
Giver-Server: Don Felder (musician), Q (*James Bond*)
Giver-Administrator: Project coordinators
Giver-Exhorter: Red Skelton (entertainer), Jerry Lewis (entertainer)

CHAPTER 7

SERVER

"Let me help you clean it up."

SERVERS are an interesting ID because they're focused on filling the needs of other people, and a lot of the time, they will act as one of the other IDs to fill that need. A Server might grab a broom and sweep up a mess, or they might point out a crooked picture like a Perceiver or explain the solution to a problem like a Teacher. They're like chameleons, and they love to help others.

Like I shared before, I'm a Compassion-Server, so I love to adjust and fill needs in my HOW, but in this chapter, we're going to hear from my favorite Server, my better half, my wife, Morgan!

Morgan and I spend most of our time serving together. We meet up in our Server HOWs to help and connect with the people around us. We get tons of energy working together, and I'm very excited for you to get the chance to meet her!

Morgan, will you help everyone get to know the Server you are?

GROWING UP

Hello everyone! My name is Morgan, and I am a Server-Server.

My mom has been an elementary school teacher for basically my whole life. Growing up, I spent a lot of time at school with her while she worked in her classroom. During the summer, I would be at school with my mom and the other teachers as they got their rooms ready for the new school year. The teachers were constantly changing and refreshing their rooms. I would go from teacher to teacher to see if I could help someone do something, anything. I really wanted to help them make their rooms nicer. The other teachers would tell my mom how helpful I was in their room makeovers. Those were the best words I could hear! I could be at school for hours and not get bored because I was helping the teachers by filling their needs. To this day, I still feel amazing when someone says I helped them with something.

WHO AM I?

Servers are very interesting Intangible Drivers because they get energy and motivation being an adjustable ID. Servers want to do whatever it takes to fill a need. A hint from the Intangible Driver quiz is when someone chooses more than two options. A Server ID will often say their response depends on the person they are with because their answer will change based on the person or need.

If someone needs to be made aware of something, the Server will move to Perceiver and begin perceiving. If the person needs understanding, the Server will move to Teacher and begin explaining the why, and so on. The Server who moves to Perceiver because there is a need gets their energy from filling the need, not actually perceiving. A Perceiver would get their energy from the actual act of perceiving.

Servers want a need to be filled so that something can be more profitable. They want people or situations to be better than they were before. I will approach pretty much any problem with any perspective to make it better. Then once the issue is fixed or the need is filled, I'm ready to move on.

My parents take a summer trip every year to the Cayman Islands. I've gone with them quite a few times, just the three of us. The first year after I got married, my husband came with us. He had never been to the Cayman Islands, so we talked about what would make the trip awesome for him. He said he wanted to have a "true Cayman experience." So my goal for the trip was to filter everything through what would be the ultimate Cayman experience. When I vacation with my parents, I can get bored because there is a lot of beach time and not a lot of "filling needs" time. So on this trip, when we would spend a few hours just sitting on the beach or floating in the ocean, I was able to look at it as helping my husband have a "true Cayman experience." Everything we did, I saw it as helping him, filling a need for him, as serving him, and it was the best trip I ever had to the Cayman Islands.

CONFIRMATION QUESTIONS

Do you have a hard time saying "No" to helping others? Because Servers are eager to fill needs, they often find themselves taking on too many projects and tasks and getting worn out. It is painful for a

Server to say no in response to a need, but it is something they need to learn if they want to avoid burnout.

Do you lose energy when you are told you *have* to do something? The kryptonite for a Server is feeling like they *have* to do something.

Would your answer to the ice cream quiz change depending on who dropped the sundae? Server HOWs adjust to the Intangible Driver of the people they interact with and can seem like chameleons. If a Server HOW interacts with a Perceiver friend, they will act like a Perceiver. If the Server interacts with an Exhorter friend, they will act like an Exhorter.

Do you think you are a Server? Do you know someone who might be a Server?

DIRECTION

Server Intangible Drivers are future-focused. They aren't *far* in the future, but they do tend to want to move forward quickly. A friend of mine asked me to share some stories from my past to explain my Intangible Driver. I sat down to work on this and felt drained. I wanted to find other things to do instead. It took me a couple of weeks to even start working on it because quickly after I agreed to do it, I moved forward to other needs. Sitting down and trying to think backward about the past does not give me energy. Thinking and planning about something in the future gives me tons of energy. I was excited thinking about sharing stories with my friend and how it would help people, but I was not excited trying to remember the past or even actually remembering the past. It was tough to remember because I was past it and on to the next thing.

This is sometimes hard on my family. When we all get together, many of them, especially those with a past-focused Intangible Driver, want to reminisce about past family events. I sometimes feel bad because I don't try hard to remember those times. If someone does the remembering and then shares the story, I appreciate it and can discuss it. I sometimes feel that I come across like I don't care, but I do. It's just that focusing on the past is more challenging for a future-focused ID.

METHOD

Servers are a DO*ing* Intangible Driver. Most often, my favorite day of the week is Saturday. On Saturdays, I create a list of all the things that I want to get done. In the morning, my husband and I get up, have some coffee and spend the next four to five hours getting things done. We go to every store, get every grocery, make food, do chores, walk around, and run all the errands. It feels awesome! Those four or five hours go by quickly, and I have so much energy to get everything done. My husband started calling them "Server Saturdays" because it was all about "doing" things.

THE WHY EFFECT

Server WHYs are "profitability junkies." A few years ago, my friends were selling their house that they had been living in for over ten years and moving into an apartment in a different city that was about a third of the size of the house. It would be a lot of work to go through all the years of accumulated stuff, decide what to keep and what to get rid of, and then pack everything up and move it. This was a huge need! For weeks, I could see all the needs and would ask my friends how the project was coming, and they would say, "Fine." It would drive me crazy! Seriously! I could see the need to organize, the need to coordinate

> **TAKING A SECOND TO EXPLAIN THE PERSPECTIVE YOU ARE COMING FROM WILL HELP OTHERS NOT BE SKEPTICAL OF YOU.**

people to help with the move, the packing that was needed, the need for trips to the thrift store or the dumpster to get rid of items that wouldn't go with them to their new home, etc., but no, they said it wasn't needed yet. I knew that was not the case, though, because it was just too big of a project.

Finally, when it was time to be out of the house, they asked for help, and I was in "go mode." I moved to Perceiver and Teacher and made sure they identified and knew what might fit in the new apartment and what would not. I moved to Administrator and ensured a crew of people was coordinated to show up and help, load up cars, and be provided directions and locations to the new apartment. I moved to Compassion and was relieved when others comforted my friends who were struggling to say goodbye to the many treasures they had collected throughout the years. I moved to Exhorter to ensure they were encouraged about their new life as empty-nesters and the pending adventure of a new job in a new town. I felt great as each need was filled.

Server WHYs are generally regarded with skepticism. People are unsure of them because they don't immediately know why they are doing what they are doing. For example, a Server-Teacher would approach every situation by teaching, yet people wouldn't understand why they are teaching. Do they want others to be aware, like a Perceiver? Do they want others to be excited like an Exhorter?

In the same way, a Server WHY is skeptical of other people because they are adjusting to the need in the moment. If a Server WHY realizes that no one has the perspective of Perceiver when looking at a problem, they take on that perspective because it is a need. Then they see four people with an Exhorter WHY hanging out with each other. If there is another need, a Server WHY will see this and think, "What are you doing? That's not what we need right now."

To help Server WHY IDs, try to see past the skepticism others have of them and ask them to share why they are doing what they are doing. Ask them what they feel the need is in the situation. This helps the Server WHY understand where they are now instead of realizing it indirectly through an interaction.

If you are a Server WHY, taking a second to explain the perspective you are coming from will help others not be skeptical of you. Luckily, there are only seven perspectives to choose from!

THE HOW CONNECTION

The Server HOW will actually fill the need, whereas the Server WHY wants the need to be filled. The Server HOWs are the ones that jump into action when a need is presented. I am a Server-Server. I shared my story about my friends moving. I was able to see the needs in my Server WHY ID and fulfill the needs in my Server HOW ID.

I was able to identify the most profitable ID needed each step of the way in my Server WHY, and I was able to fill each of the needs in my Server HOW. When I can do both with the most profitable outcome, I feel like a Superwoman.

Another way a Server HOW can fill a need is to sync up with the HOW of another person. If a Compassion WHY-Server HOW wants to fill needs, and they are with a Perceiver WHY-Teacher HOW, the Compassion-Server can move their Server HOW to Teacher so that the two of them can fill the teaching need together. However, the

Perceiver-Teacher is teaching to make the other person aware of something the Perceiver-Teacher has perceived. The Compassion-Server is teaching because the need is teaching. The Compassion-Server wants to bear the pain of the person being taught.

Server HOWs are generally seen as likable. They change based on the HOW position of other Intangible Drivers, so they are excellent connectors. A Perceiver HOW will say that a Server HOW is like him. Likewise, an Exhorter HOW can think a Server HOW is like him, yet the Perceiver and Exhorter know they are not like each other at all. Nearly every superhero we see in movies has a Server HOW, and they use it to connect with others.

HOW TO HELP

Servers love to fill needs and help other people. Do you know what we want to hear more than anything else? "I need help."

We will jump into action when we hear that, but how often do you think we hear that? When was the last time you told someone, "I need help."?

Often, people don't want to risk sharing that they need help because they fear it will make them sound weak or not up to the task themselves. So when they do ask for help, they tend to boss others around. "Sweep the floor." or, "Can you wash the dishes today?"

I always find it funny when the parents of Server children tell the kids the chores they *have to do* that day. Telling the kids they *have to* is the quickest way to guarantee that the task won't get done. If the parent were to express the need for help, the Server kids would be quicker to help.

What motivates me is when I hear someone share their needs. So the advice I give to those parents is to share their needs like they're just talking to an empty room. "I'm trying to cook dinner, but I need help getting these dishes washed!" The Servers in the room will jump up and start washing the dishes.

My husband is a Compassion-Server. We often struggle when deciding where to eat because we both want to fill the need and adjust to the other in our Server HOWs. We can be heard saying, "Well, what are you hungry for tonight?" "I don't know. What do you want to eat?" "I could go for whatever. What's your favorite food?" This could go on for hours, or worse, lead to frustration. We've learned that one of us needs to decide to have a strong opinion. Once we've identified that we are stuck in a Server loop, one of us will suggest something, like, "How about Italian?" And then we go out for Italian food.

MISUNDERSTOOD

A few years ago, I was at a friend's house meeting with a group of women. We were sitting around talking and sharing when one of the women came into the room and let one of the other women know that her son just threw up downstairs. The mother quickly got up and ran downstairs to check on her son, while another person got some supplies to help clean things up.

As I continued to sit and focus on the group that was there for the meeting, one of the women turned to me and asked why I didn't help with the sick kid. To me, the need was already filled, so I didn't feel like I needed to be the one to step in and do more. In fact, I thought the need was to continue to focus and go forward with the group still there.

Often Server WHYs are compared to Server HOWs in that they want to be the person to fill every need, but the Server WHY steps back to see what need would be the ultimate effect.

We saw Server WHYs are generally regarded with skepticism.

> **IF SERVERS DON'T HAVE ANY NEEDS TO FILL, THEY TEND TO GO LOOKING FOR THEM...**

People are unsure of them because they don't immediately know why they are doing what they are doing. If a Server WHY thinks someone needs to be made aware of an issue and starts to Perceive on that person, others watching may wonder why the Server WHY is perceiving. And because they don't know why the person needed to be made aware of some issue, the bystander may think the Server WHY is controlling, naive, or negative.

The way to handle the situation is to simply ask the Server WHY why they are trying to make the person aware of an issue. Why are they perceiving? Alternatively, it's a benefit for Server WHYs to grow in their ability to share with others what they believe is the need. For example, at work, I often explain why I've asked for information in my emails to people or in meetings so they know why I'm saying what I'm saying. This helps eliminate the skepticism.

Also, when the Server HOW is adjusting to those around them and seemingly acting like a chameleon, others might think they are being fake or have no personality. A Server HOW can act like the other Intangible Drivers, and their unique personality comes in how they adjust to the need by acting in the ID that is needed.

Another way to misunderstand a Server is to think they are busybodies. For the past few years, I've been serving on a committee. Recently, I've been looking to come off the committee, but I'm waiting for a replacement to be named. So when I got an email from the committee leader about a new process he was implementing, I thought it didn't make sense, and there was a better way of doing it.

I reached out and started asking questions to clarify and understand what he was doing and why. I began to feel unsettled and annoyed with the interaction, so I reached out to my husband for some advice. My husband asked me if I wanted to get more involved with this committee or be off the committee. I had determined I did not want to get more involved. In fact, I was trying to be less involved. It was then that I realized I was being a busybody. As a Server, I can pull myself into every situation because I can always feel like there is a need or a way it can be more profitable, even when there isn't, or it's not my responsibility.

If Servers don't have any needs to fill, they tend to go looking for them, which results in them appearing to be busybodies. It can also result in Servers taking on various new projects that they may never have time to complete.

Servers are motivated to fill the needs of others. There are two keywords: *needs* and *others*. The need has to be about someone else. Often, a Server will be unmotivated to do something until they believe it is a need. This can lead to Servers being procrastinators and only wanting to do something when it's their idea. When a Server isn't presented with a need or is presented something for their own benefit, they lose their energy and motivation.

The most significant way a Server can be mistreated is to tell them they *have to* do something. It's the worst possible way that they would have to do something for themselves. If I say to a Server, "You need to drive me to the gas station because my car broke down on the way here," they may lose their energy and have no desire to help me. A Server who feels like *they have to do something* will be completely drained. If I were to say instead, "My car broke down on the way here, and I need a ride to the gas station," a Server will instantly have energy and *want* to help me.

UNHEALTHY USE OF ID

If a Server is in an unhealthy state of mind, they may start to see opportunities to fill needs as situations where they *have to* fill the need. They begin to feel like they are in serfdom, and they can lash out.

There was a time when the house I lived at was the go-to hangout house for a large group of my friends. Every weekend, about ten to fifteen people would come over and spend almost the entire day there. We would watch movies, hang out on the deck in the backyard, play volleyball, and just sit around and talk. People knew that the house was "open" for anyone and everyone to come over whenever and that people would always be around. With the excitement of people coming over, I started making food every week. I loved getting to provide a meal for everyone, and I loved hosting! After months of making these meals, people would start asking, "So, what's for dinner?" That's when I began to get upset.

One Saturday, while hanging out with friends, dinner time was approaching, and someone asked, "Morgan, what's for dinner?" I was pissed! I stormed off to the car to drive to the grocery store so I could figure out what to make for dinner to feed these "free-loaders"! My boyfriend at the time came with me and asked me, "What's wrong?". I started to share with him how I felt like people now expect me to cook every week. I felt the pull on the pocket strings for the cost of providing food, the time it took, especially if it meant I couldn't hang out with everyone because I was in the kitchen, and that people didn't even appreciate it or want the food that I made. But I also felt that I *had* to make the food - it was expected, and people would be upset at me if I didn't make food for everyone. As we talked through how I was feeling, he helped me see that people had the option and ability to get their own food. Asking "what's for dinner" might be someone trying to determine what the plan for the rest of the night is, and if there weren't a food plan, then maybe they would come up with one and offer to make food.

From there, he asked me if making food was something that I wanted to do before anyone asked, "what's for dinner?" - which I did. He assured me that I didn't have to make food for everyone and asked if I still wanted to make food, at least that day. To which I did. Going forward, I most often wanted to cook every week still, though sometimes, I would ask if other people also wanted to help or even pitch in some money; and people were more than eager to contribute!

RELATIONSHIPS

Servers get along very well with Compassion because Servers tend to take on too much and get overwhelmed. Compassion wants to relieve that pain, and they also like that Servers are focused on the benefit of other people.

Administrators and Servers often get along very well as long as the Administrator is focusing on helping the group or an individual in the group. As soon as they turn the focus on assisting the Server, the Server stops getting energy.

Servers tend to avoid Teacher IDs because Teachers tend to commentate without end, whether it's a need or not. A Server will eventually feel the need is filled and want them to stop talking!

CHILDREN: PARENTING AND TEACHING

We believe half of the people in the world are Server HOW and half are not. The most essential first step a parent ought to take towards their child is to determine if they are Server HOW or not. The non-Server

> **MOST PEOPLE HAVE A NATURAL SKILL FOR A FEW THINGS AND TEND TO FOCUS ON JUST THOSE THINGS.**

HOW children seem to be ambitious, yet they don't get along with other children. The Server HOW children seem to be tough to motivate and cause parents to think they will try to get through life relying on their personality.

Server HOW children are hard to motivate because telling them what to do, especially with a focus on how it would benefit them, tends to demotivate the child. Then the parent thinks they have to ramp up the motivation techniques, which further drain the child. Eventually, the parent will make the child so uncomfortable, the child is "motivated," and the parent says, "See what they make me do to them." Actually, stating the need would have caused half of children to be motivated.

Server WHY children present an entirely different challenge. One of the ways I see a person's WHY is as "glasses" they wear. A Perceiver WHY wears Perceiver glasses that show them what is wrong. A Compassion WHY wears Compassion glasses that show them who is in pain. A Server WHY can wear any of the seven glasses. In fact, they can switch glasses between sentences! This is because Server WHYs can see all the way around an issue. They see all seven perspectives!

Server WHY children can be seen as argumentative and stubborn. Why? They have seven reasons why they believe what they believe. They can sound like they are repeating themselves by saying the same thing seven times. In reality, they are saying the same thing from different perspectives. When you convince them they are wrong with one reason, the child still thinks they are right because it is 6 to 1. To persuade and motivate Server WHYs, you need to have at least four reasons why you are correct so that it is 4 to 3 in your favor.

CAREERS

Servers tend to be naturally talented in a lot of different areas. They pick up the first part of a skill quickly, going from 0-70% in record time, but they then see another skill they could learn, and they go towards getting that one from 0-70%.

Most people have a natural skill for a few things and tend to focus on just those things. Over time they bring their skill from 0-100% and become experts in that skill. Servers tend to get a lot of areas to 70% and then move on. This can be a struggle for people who work with Servers because it can seem like the Server is just naturally good at everything. Over time, Servers may start to feel lost and unsure if they are good at anything because their non-Server friends begin to excel in one area, and the Server hasn't been able to decide what "one" area they want to focus on.

Servers need to learn that they also have a "one thing" like everyone else. Servers can build diverse skills so quickly that they are perfect for fields that act as a bridge between experts.

Job choices may include support services such as maintenance, coordinators, administration, firefighters, and guest services.

Often, you'll see Servers in job fields like maintenance, which is the bridge between a business owner, a machine operator, and an engineering staff. A talented maintenance technician ends up working with every part of a manufacturing business and is pretty good at all of them but isn't an expert in any of them.

There is even a fairly new profession to describe a Server who works in engineering, which is traditionally a field that tends to be filled with Teachers and not Servers. The term is Engineering Technologist. They're involved in everything from engineering to sales, focusing on serving needs anywhere along the workflow path.

Technicians need to be able to fit in with all of the roles involved. They can work with engineers to solve problems. They can discuss long-term machine health in terms of business opportunities with managers. They can do welding and machining to create solutions to issues physically. They can work with the various people operating machines every day. Servers are the glue that holds organizations together.

Servers tend to fit perfectly into careers that are a summation of the different skills they've developed. Educators are another perfect example. Educators in K-12 need to be good enough at their subject matter to teach it. They need to be adept at communicating verbally. Through writing, they need to be good at collecting data and communicating with parents. They need to tell stories, mediate problems, and deal with all kinds of different people daily. The majority of grade school teachers are Servers.

Instead of worrying about being an expert at a particular skill, if you are a Server, try to think about how your skills can add up. That might help you decide on what it is you want to do in a profession.

SELF HELP

How can a Server overcome this feeling of being drained in a world full of people telling them what to do?

A man decides that he wants to cook a nice dinner for his wife that evening after work, but as he leaves the house in the morning, his wife says to him, "You have to cook dinner tonight because I have a doctor's appointment."

The man feels immediately drained and unmotivated when his wife tells him he has to cook dinner, even though he wanted to just minutes before she said anything. How does he get his energy back?

He could ask himself if he wanted to cook dinner before she told him he had to cook. If he can get back to the original desire, his energy returns as he remembers that he was actually going to fill her need, not his own.

CHEAT SHEET

Server-Perceiver
Wants to make people aware of an issue to fill a need. "This mess needs to be cleaned up."

Server-Teacher
Wants to help people understand why an issue exists to fill a need. "That small plate caused the sundae to fall and make this mess."

Server-Compassion
Wants to bear the emotional pain of people to fill a need. "Don't worry about cleaning this up. I'll do it."

Server-Giver
Wants to give a tangible gift or improvement to people to fill a need. "Let me clean this up for you."

Server-Server
Wants to fill a need to fill a need. "Let me help you clean this up."

Tip: Server-Server is a particular case, so let's take a moment to look at them more closely.

When it comes to the ID quiz, if a person becomes visibly upset at the thought of taking the quiz, you can assume they are Server-Server. They have unconsciously learned that no personality test is going to be able to cover all the effects of forty-nine contexts (seven WHY IDs times seven HOW IDs).

Whenever people test out as Compassion-Server or Giver-Server, we try to take the extra step to see if they are Server-Server.

Half of the time, people like Server-Servers, and the other half of the time, they are skeptical. Server-Servers can do anything, so they tend not to do anything at a world-class level. They are the proverbial "Jack of all trades, master of none." They spend a lot of time going in one direction and then doubting themselves because they could just as easily go in one or two other directions. They tend to get depressed as teenagers because they see everyone beginning to grow in a specific area and earn respect, while they have no idea what they want to do because they can do anything.

Since a Server-Server can get energy doing anything (they are forty-nine people after all), they think they have to be the best at everything. This is the superhuman syndrome. This is why it is crucial for a Server-Server to determine what their one thing is. Once they've done this, they can focus on being the best at everything connected with that one thing, and they can allow themselves not to have to be the best at everything else.

Server HOWs can be seen as an adapter with seven outlets. They deliver their specific WHY through seven channels. Server WHYs can be seen as seven power sources that deliver their WHY through one channel. Server-Server is a multi-use adapter with seven sources and seven deliveries. This makes Server-Servers the ultimate at connecting people, to the point they don't seem to have an intrinsic purpose. They are entirely focused on helping a person connect to another person through themselves.

In groups of four or fewer, Server-Servers tend to be extroverts. They act as a bridge between people by adjusting back and forth in both their WHY and HOW so that the other people feel connected, no matter their Intangible Driver.

Organizations with a ratio of 1:4 Server to non-Server IDs tend to thrive quickly because the Servers facilitate a quick connection between others. This allows everyone to be able to get along and work well together.

In groups of five or more, Servers tend to start acting like an introvert because they have so many options to adjust to that they become overwhelmed. They have a hard time figuring out where to adjust or what needs to fill, so they simply do nothing.

Server-Administrator
Wants to coordinate a group of people to fill a need. "I'll help you clean this up by having Ted and Marcia get some napkins. Ted and Marcia, let's clean this up."

Server-Exhorter
Wants to encourage people about the future to fill a need. "This will be fun to clean up!"

FAMOUS EXAMPLES OF SERVER-WHYS

Server-Perceiver: Pam Beasley (TV show *The Office*), John Lennon (musician)
Server-Teacher: Bill Gates (Founder of Microsoft), Vince Lombardi (NFL football coach)
Server-Compassion: Mr. Rogers, Emotional and Behavioral Disorder Teachers
Server-Giver: Thomas Edison
Server-Server: Aragorn (book/movie *The Lord of the Rings*), Katniss Everdeen (*The Hunger Games*), Superman, Harry Potter (book/movie *Harry Potter*)
Server-Administrator: Bill Belichek (NFL football coach)
Server-Exhorter: Leaders at a pep rally

CHAPTER 8

ADMINISTRATOR

"Susan, get the waitress. Jim, pick up the glass. Ted, grab some napkins."

IN THIS chapter, we're going to learn about the Administrator Intangible Driver. Administrators see the world in a unique way because they see individuals in terms of a group. Administrators are always trying to help move people around to get them in the proper position so that a group of people can make progress towards a goal. I love it when I get to be part of a winning team, so I'm eager to listen to the Administrators in my life.

We're going to be hearing from my friend Ben in this chapter. Ben is a musician, and when we get together to play music, I want Ben to direct me in how I play because I know he's going to get us moving together towards making some incredible music. It's always fun when I let Ben act like himself, and I hope you can learn how to let the Administrators in your life lead you from his story.

Ben, will you lead us?

GROWING UP

Hello, my name is Ben, and my Intangible Driver is Administrator.

When I was very young, I loved playing with my toys and making up stories. I think back to those days, and I noticed that the stories were always the same concept. I would create unique characteristics in four to five toys, and they would work together to fight the bad guys. I would model one of the characters after myself, and he would always be the leader of the group. Even when I would play games with my friends, they always looked to me for the rules to explain what was happening in the make-believe world I created and explain their abilities. I loved it!

As I grew up, I wanted to administrate more and more, but I found that the adults in my life always shut down opportunities. Looking back, I understand what they were doing as no one wants to be told what to do by a kid. But this caused me to feel like there were fewer opportunities to be myself.

My teachers could have used me to help get a class organized if they had given me the goal, but they would have had to give up some control. That's hard for many adults to do with a kid, and it resulted in me having very few outlets to administrate, which meant very few outlets to be myself.

What do you think I did? Do you think I sat patiently for years until I was a grown man that people would let direct a group towards something profitable?

Of course not. I started administrating anything that I could. If my teachers and parents kept shutting down the opportunities for me to administrate in a helpful way, what avenue do you think was left for me to be myself? Exactly. Trouble. I started administrating trouble.

In every grade, there are kids who don't want to do the work and would rather mess around than follow the teachers' instruction, but they were always sloppy and disorganized. If they had someone directing them, they might actually be able to get away with screwing around a little more. My only outlet for administrating turned into administrating a group of kids, like me, to go towards goals that would end up getting us in trouble.

I could administrate the group to sneak out at night and hang out at a friend's house, playing video games instead of doing our homework. Everyone was tired the next day, and our grades suffered, but for a night, I got to be myself.

I could administrate the group on how to pass notes and text during class so that we could still talk behind the teacher's back without them knowing. We struggled on our tests, and some of us got detention, but for a few brief moments, I got to be myself.

I have a lot of empathy for kids growing up as an Administrator. No one lets them administrate, and they become desperate for opportunities to be themselves. They'd love to help, but if the only way to be themselves is to be destructive, they're going to do that instead.

When I see those kids, I try to help them administrate something good and profitable so that they can learn how to be themselves without getting hurt or getting others hurt.

> IN EVERY GRADE, THERE ARE KIDS WHO DON'T WANT TO DO THE WORK AND WOULD RATHER MESS AROUND.

WHO AM I

Administrators are focused on the group or the interactions between people. It seems so simple now when I look back on my childhood. My toys would always let me administrate them. My close friends wanted me to put them in a role, and I believe it is because they knew I was an Administrator and wanted to be led towards a goal.

I believe some of the only people I didn't get along with when I was younger were other Administrators because we would compete over who would get to administrate the other.

Once I understood that I am an Administrator, I realized why people looked to me for direction; why they looked to me as a leader. Now I realize that if I had worked together with the other Administrator kids, we could have done more of what we wanted together. But you'd probably never get us to shut up individually about how awesome our strategy was.

Looking back on those times, I realize that the way I've always seen the world is by looking at the connections between people. When I see a group of five people, I see one body made up of five points, and if those points are aligned the wrong way, the whole group flounders, and no one has a good time. I can see how if we just move two people around, then everyone would have a better time. This constantly happens to me, and I can't turn it off.

When I look at an individual, I see the connection between where they are now and the future version of themselves. I want to bring those points together, which is why I want to hear people's goals. I want to connect them with their future! When I learned this about myself, I felt settled because I struggle to relate to people who don't want to do anything. People who have no ambition frustrate me because the future version of themselves isn't different. What would I connect those people to? They're already where they want to be.

CONFIRMATION QUESTIONS

Are you listless until you have a goal? Do you get energized helping a group towards a goal? Do you get energized helping a person be a part of a group?

Do you think you are an Administrator? Who do you know that might be an Administrator?

DIRECTION

Administrators are focused on the future. I look at how I can coordinate a group towards a goal that is in front of us.

I was working with a band several years ago before I learned I was an Administrator. One beautiful spring morning, I remember walking to our practice site, and I was working out a new idea based on one of the band member's riffs from the jam session the previous night. I was starting to see how we could include each band member in this new piece that would absolutely top off our entire set. I was so full of energy and felt on top of the world.

I started to share the new idea, and as I introduced and included each band member in his part, I could see the vision get closer and closer. My energy grew and grew, and I was actually becoming excited.

As I was helping the drummer with his part, our manager came in and wanted us to discuss our experience playing at a venue we had played about three weeks ago. Within minutes, I could feel all the energy drain out of me. I became quiet and lethargic. Our manager became frustrated because he thought it was a perfect time to talk to us. After all, we were so full of energy minutes before, and he thought it could be a fun discussion with all of us so pumped up. He asked me if he had done something to offend me.

I reflected on my reaction for several days. How could I go from this amazing feeling and completely synced up with the band to a sense of being in the dumps within minutes, over something that was reasonable for our manager to ask us? I felt I had disappointed our manager, who has done so much for us. How could I be so disrespectful?

When I learned I was an Administrator, a tremendous weight was lifted off my shoulders. I realized that I'm future-focused, and the act of having to remember the past is simply the opposite of my Intangible Driver. I can remember the past, but it doesn't get me excited like moving a group towards the future. From then on, when asked to remember details about the past, I would recognize it was something that needed to be done, and it would simply feel like a chore. I now knew that the draining feeling wasn't a sign I was a bad person or that the person asking for past information is bad. Whew!

METHOD

Administrators coordinate a group towards a goal through speaking. Sometimes, I get incredibly nervous that I talk too much. A friend shared with me recently that she was having a blast filling out quizzes and reading articles about what to do on vacation: ziplining, parasailing, snorkeling, and so on. There are so many things to DO on vacation. In my opinion, there are not enough vacation tips for someone like me, the guy who wants to sit at a table in a bar with three interesting people instead of finding out what dolphin skin feels like (exactly how you'd imagine it probably).

But, there was a time when my friends asked me to go down one of those inflatable tube water rides. I said no at first and was ready to move on, but then they asked me if I would do it if we all raced against each other. Well, they reached me! Of course, I would do it for a group with a goal. I didn't win a single race, and I didn't care. It was a group with a goal, so I had a blast!

An Administrator can get frustrated if their words are not resulting in the group moving. Excellent Administrators become masters of words and masters of influence. Being able to clearly communicate the vision, the benefit to each person involved, and give clear instructions will often result in the goal being achieved.

THE WHY EFFECT

As an Administrator WHY, I want to influence others. I want people to move together under the same sun. I ultimately want to help other people find their position in relation to their goals. Administrator WHYs like to sit back and have a good time once the group is working together, which causes them to appear to be everyone's buddy.

At the end of most of our band practices, we would keep everything plugged in because now it was time to just jam. I knew each of the band members wanted just to flow. They needed a vision to sync up with to be their authentic self and flow and create.

I would tell the drummer, "give us a beat," and then, as soon as he would start, I would look at the guitarist and yell out a chord structure. We would play for hours, and it felt like minutes. I would get so much energy from directing the music and helping each band member achieve their place in the vision that I was even completely fine with packing up all my heavy equipment, even though it is something I hated doing.

In all honesty, if I wasn't allowed to direct my band, and all I could do is pack everything up or teach someone how my equipment works, I would have quit that band the very same day I joined it.

I just want to joke around and create with a group. I don't get energy focusing on the needs, the individuals, the understanding, none of it, even though I know all of those are important. My fun is syncing people up towards their goal. That's it.

There is a young girl who goes to my church. At the end of each service, she always wants to help clean up the sound equipment. I knew that she was an Administrator and that she barely had a single opportunity to administrate anything because no one knew how to interact with her. So, when she would help clean up, I would show her how to clean up two to three things, have her do it, and then move on. Finally, after a few weeks of her helping, two other kids joined, and I looked at her and asked, "Is there anything these other kids can do?" She lit up and started asking the kids to do all of the work that I showed her! I administrated her to administrate those kids. Double win!

There are many classic movies where an Administrator comes to town and cleans up a colossal mess, only to leave the moment the goal has been achieved. They're off to find the next town that needs something accomplished.

A fantastic example of this is the Man with No Name from A Fistfull of Dollars. Played by a young Clint Eastwood, the Man with No Name enters a lonely town where two rival cartels are feuding. He finds out that the townsfolk are suffering greatly because of this and begins to play both sides against each other.

He successfully gets the gangs to shoot each other out over a chest of gold, to raid one another over a kidnapped woman, and when one cartel finally wins out over the other, he takes out the leaders of the winning cartel.

After saving the town from these two rival gangs, he could be celebrated as a hero, but instead, he rides away from the town in search of a new problem to solve.

THE HOW CONNECTION

Administrator HOWs want to coordinate others towards a goal for the sake of the goal. If a goal is set at a company to bring in ten new clients over the next month, the Administrator HOW will start moving people around to accomplish the goal, whether the people want to achieve the goal or not. That is different from the Administrator WHY, who wants to help others towards their goals.

Administrator HOWs see the group as an individual itself. If I wanted to cross the street, every part of my body would need to be working together to get me across. My eyes would look for cars coming. My feet would have to be pointed in the right direction. My muscles would have to work to move me.

Can you imagine if my head was turned looking behind me, and my feet were both pointing different ways, and my muscles refused to propel me forward? Do you think I'm going to make it across the street? An Administrator HOW sees all the parts of the whole and how each has to move to achieve the goal collectively.

HOW TO HELP

I cannot stress enough that an Administrator is motivated by a goal. If you want to get along with an Administrator, the first step is to share your goals.

Do you remember reading in the Compassion chapter about how Compassion can appear awkward until they know what someone is feeling?

Administrators can seem disinterested until they know the goal. It can be challenging for people to understand, but an integral part of who an Administrator is involves seeing people based on their connection to

> **GIVE AN ADMINISTRATOR SOMETHING TO WORK WITH, AND THEY WILL HELP YOU CONQUER THE WORLD.**

others in a group or their future goal. If we don't see those connections, we don't know how to interact with someone.

The big difference is that while Compassion is very concerned about causing pain, resulting in awkward behavior, Administrators are not concerned about causing pain. We don't know how to talk to a person with no connections to other people or a goal, so we just don't engage.

I have Administrator friends who will ask a few questions when they meet someone. They'll ask about work, they'll ask about family, they'll ask about friends, and when people give completely superficial answers to those questions, like, "Work is work. Family is fine. Friends are alright." I can see the Administrator steadily go from excited about meeting this new person to completely drained and unsure of what to say.

Give an Administrator something to work with, and they will help you conquer the world.

However, it is very common for people to be unsure of taking direction from another person, which means when the Administrator tries to help them, someone could feel like they're being controlled or manipulated. How can you tell if you're working with an administrator trying to help you get to your dreams or working with a manager who is trying to schmooze you into doing what they want you to do?

All you have to ask is one simple question. "How will this help the group move towards our goal?"

If they avoid that question, they're likely trying to move the group to benefit themselves. But if they can answer it, then you can feel safe trusting their direction.

MISUNDERSTOOD

Administrators are energized to work *with* you and help you get everything sorted out to accomplish a goal. As soon as you've reached the goal, they lose interest. In the same way, an Administrator can seem like they care about all of the people in a group while the group is together having an enjoyable time. However, as soon as the Administrator is one on one with a member of that group, they lose interest if they don't actually care for that person. This can cause Administrators to be misunderstood as uncaring and cruel because others can feel like there was an individual connection, while the Administrator was actually feeling a connection with the group as a whole.

That's not to say that Administrators don't have connections with individuals. It's just that they can *seem* connected when they aren't because they are energized towards a group or to help with a goal.

Because I am trying to move others towards a goal, some people see me as bossy, controlling, or a "game player," especially if they don't understand the goal. They can feel I'm trying to move them, and it can feel uncomfortable if not understood. I'm sure there were many times I was trying to move people because I wanted them to move towards my goal, but as I have matured, I want to help others move towards their goals, so I am often misunderstood. I am genuinely trying to help them, and I get so much energy when I can help them achieve their goals.

I had a friend who wanted help with confronting her boss at work who was treating her disrespectfully. I got excited by this goal and began to give advice and coaching on how she could confront her boss successfully. She listened to my advice and then went on with her week. She later shared a couple of stories where she could have confronted her boss but didn't. I asked her why she didn't take my advice, and she told me she felt I was just trying to prove a point with my advice and control her. I explained I only wanted to help her with her goal of confrontation, and when she understood and felt I was indeed for her and her goal, she went into her next week, intending to use my advice. It was great!

Another way I have been misunderstood is when I don't have a goal, I can become listless and apathetic. I can seem like I'm just wandering without purpose. Others have often seen this in me and have accused me of being lazy and that I don't care. My bosses at work can think I'm a lousy employee even when I have actively sought to understand the goal of what we as a team are trying to accomplish. When my bosses can't tell me the goal, I struggle. I've learned that if those in authority can't help me clearly understand the goal, I need to seek others who can help me. Even mini-goals can keep me motivated.

UNHEALTHY USE OF ID

When an Administrator tries to act for their own benefit, it is usually because they are trying to get a plan to work, and there is just one person or thing in their way. Therefore, it can be very easy for an Administrator to justify misleading someone to get that plan to work.

Administrators are the other Intangible Driver (along with Perceivers) that tend to get in trouble during their school years. This is because, before graduation, it is rare for adults to let Administrators administrate anything because they are too young. Consequently, they end up coordinating their classmates in the only way available... trouble. The Administrator often won't *do* anything themselves, but when the teachers finally untangle the web of chaos, they find the Administrator at the center of it all and punish them.

I started lying to people about my life in elementary school. I wanted everyone to come towards me, think I was the most unique and interesting person, and love me. I kept lying to everyone to get them to do what I wanted, to move where I saw fit. I was misleading everyone around me to commit crimes, rip people off, and talk poorly about others. It was all for the sake of my low self-esteem and wanting to feel that I was a bigger and better person, and I felt that momentarily by tearing others down. People got in a lot of trouble, even arrested, due to my words and my misdirection. My words were of anarchy and destruction but said through a message of peace, and I had so many convinced what they were doing, even hurting others, was for a good cause. No bit of it was worth the pain I watched others go through or the pain I went through.

People getting hurt or arrested is the most extreme example I have in my life of misusing my Administrator ID, but there are plenty of examples of me misusing my ability to direct a group that don't involve a supervillain level of destruction. One such example is how I used to handle my music.

I've wanted to be a musician ever since I was young because there is no high for me like being in a group of people who want to jam together and create something beautiful. There is no greater high for me than to be part of that group, but in the past, I've tried to use my ability to coordinate a group of people by trying to administrate a creative environment centered around one common theme: me.

I would get my bandmates going in the direction that I wanted to go, towards my goals, to feel like I was an important person in charge of something. I tried to get an entire group of people to cure my own lack of self-esteem. If someone started to dislike the direction we were going, it was a simple matter of administrating them out of the group.

This was never fulfilling because taking control is never a cure for self-esteem. I had to learn how to use my administrator to act as a leader. Instead of manipulating and controlling others, I had to use my abilities to help them.

Now when I work in a band, I focus on administrating our efforts to maximize the entire group's experience instead of just maximizing my experience. It's more rewarding, I still get to feel the high of administrating, and I feel like I'm a strength to the people around me instead of a villain.

RELATIONSHIPS

An Administrator has a hard time feeling settled if they are focused on anything other than helping a group work or helping someone towards a goal. The easiest way to motivate an Administrator is to tell them your goal.

Typically, Administrators don't have a problem with any of the other Intangible Drivers because they know every uniqueness is necessary to get the group to be profitable.

However, Compassion IDs can have a problem with Administrators when they realize that the Administrator doesn't necessarily care about the individuals. The Compassion person would feel like the Administrator is causing pain by *not* caring.

Servers often get along very well with Administrators because the Administrator will naturally point the Server towards someone else in the group. This gives the Server a need to fill for someone else, and they feel energized. If the Administrator doesn't know better, they will tell the Server to do something for the Server themself, and the Server will lose energy. If the Administrator doesn't care for that individual Server, they will move on because, from their perspective, the Server suddenly doesn't want to work as part of the group and doesn't have any goals. This relationship causes the Administrator to look like a supervillain to the Server because both of them were drained by the interaction, and the Administrator suddenly appeared to stop caring.

Administrators also get along very well with Perceivers. An Administrator believes if they move the right pieces to the right places, they can accomplish goals. So, when something goes wrong, they feel like they were just missing a bit of information. Perceivers will point out reality without hesitation, which helps the Administrator move people to the right spot.

CAREERS

Administrators tend to fill the occupations related to coordinating a group and directing teams such as coaches, directors, generals, and managers.

If you are a manager, it is vital to ensure you understand the organization's mission, vision, values, and goals to efficiently and effectively administrate the team and groups towards it. An analogy often used by organizations is that leadership needs to ensure the right people are on the bus, in the right seat, and the bus is pointed and moving in the right direction towards the overall mission and vision. Administrators can be the perfect ID to ensure the right team members are on the bus and are all in the right seat. They can ensure those team members are all moving in the right direction at the right pace. They can see the whole group moving as one unit.

That is truly the strength of the Administrator to see the parts connected as a whole. A football coach can see the quarterback, center, running backs, fullback, wide receivers, tight end, right and left guard, and right and left tackle as parts of the whole offense. The coach can see how each of those parts needs to operate to have the entire offense achieve its goal of moving the football down the field to score a touchdown.

A director can see how each actors' role and the interaction of the roles bring a story to life. Without a director, the actors would just sound like they were auditioning for a part. The audience would have no idea how that part relates or understand the story.

A general can see the enemy's movements and how to align the troops to defend or advance on the enemy to achieve the goal of protecting a people or territory or thwarting the plans of the enemy. Because of the large scale and danger of a military mission, the troops are taught to obey their leadership on command. They understand they are being administrated and know they need to move in concert, or people can be hurt. A commander sees all the parts as an extensive system. If the recon troops go first into a new area to explore and gain information and don't follow the commander's orders, the next wave of troops could be put in harm's way. The type of troop and timing of each troop is critical to the whole mission.

An Administrator ID could get energy taking on these roles.

CHILDREN: PARENTING AND TEACHING

During the quiz, we ask potential Administrators if they got in trouble during school, not because they did something wrong, but because they got someone else to do something wrong. Whenever we ask an Administrator this question, they always laugh.

We've commonly observed young Administrators playing very violent team-based online video games. Their parents are concerned about the level of violence in the game and try to get the Administrator to do something else.

However, while playing the game, the Administrator has an opportunity to get the winning shot but tells the rest of their team that the winning shot isn't necessary to them. It isn't about them being the All-Star or the MVP of the team. The Administrator wants to direct the group, and as long as they get to do that, they are settled. Once parents realize this, they feel better because they realize they aren't raising a lunatic attracted to violence. Their kid just wants to direct a group and, for kids, video games tend to be an outlet. Parents and teachers often find success when they find healthy alternatives to allow a young Administrator to administrate.

> THE ADMINISTRATOR WANTS TO DIRECT THE GROUP, AND AS LONG AS THEY GET TO DO THAT, THEY ARE SETTLED.

Administrator children are obsessed with two things: being in the group and the one person who is outside the group. Administrators hate being the only person left out of a group. Administrators will spend all their time in the group looking at the one person who is outside the group. If an Administrator child has a hard time focusing, it could be because the setting isn't made up of an inclusive group.

Since Administrator children aren't allowed to act in their uniqueness, they are often confused with Server and Exhorter. The Server confusion comes because Administrators will fill in any role needed for the group's goals to be achieved. Notice, they don't intrinsically enjoy the role. They enjoy being a part of the group achieving its goal. Later, when the parents remember how much energy the Administrator got doing the role, they try to get him to do it again, and they are confused as to why he hates doing it.

Administrators can demonstrate wide swings in emotions like Exhorters. When the group is achieving their goal, they are the most energized person in the world. When there is no goal to achieve, they have zero energy.

Remember, Administrator children live their lives being denied their uniqueness, so it comes out sideways. I like to give children the following speech (but it also works for adults):

"Do you like to move people around?"
(They usually clam up thinking there is a hidden camera.)

"I like moving people around.
(Their eyes get wide because they can't believe I admitted it.)

"People like to be moved around!"
(This is when they will admit they are an Administrator after checking to see if anyone else can hear.)

"Everyone likes to be moved around differently. People will let you move them around one time, and if you don't move them around the way they like, they won't let you ever do it again."
(Remember, Administrators hate the idea of living a life without people to administrate.)

"However, if you move people the way they want to be moved, they will ask you to move them again!"
(This is when the Administrator's face lights up.)

"Would you like to learn how to figure out how people want to be moved?"
(THAT is what this book is about. If you have an Administrator friend, I highly recommend telling them about this book!)

SELF HELP

Administrators need to ensure they understand the goal of the group they are trying to help. If there is no known goal for the overall group, the Administrator can set mini-goals to stay energized.

Administrators should become masters at getting to know other people and excellent at communicating so that others feel good about being administrated towards a goal. Of all the people that ought to be an expert at determining the IDs of others, Administrators are at the top. They require this ability because it ultimately facilitates their uniqueness.

CHEAT SHEET

Administrator-Perceiver
Wants to make people aware of an issue to coordinate a group of people towards a goal. "We need to clean up this mess."

Notice, this is a tough ID to relate to because a Perceiver HOW means everything from Perceiver through Administrator! "We need to clean up this mess" *means*:

- *the ice cream sundae fell (Teacher)*
- *someone could get hurt slipping on this (Compassion)*
- *they are going to need another sundae (Giver)*
- *this needs to get done now (Server)*

If someone restates any of these points or asks about them instead of accomplishing the goal, the

Administrator-Perceiver can feel misunderstood. A lot of Administrator-Perceivers say they only want to work with excellent people. What they *mean* is they want to work with people who will instantly clean up the mess, keep others safe, and buy the person another sundae in response to "We need to clean up this mess." They don't want to have to explain themselves because they feel they already said all of that.

Administrator-Teacher
Wants to help people understand why an issue exists to coordinate a group of people towards a goal. "If we work together, it won't take long to clean up."

Administrator-Compassion
Wants to bear the emotional pain of others to coordinate a group of people towards a goal. "Don't worry, Ted and Marcia will help me clean this up."

Administrator-Giver
Wants to give a tangible gift or improvement to people to coordinate a group of people towards a goal. "Ted, here's some money. Buy another sundae."

Administrator-Server
Wants to fill a need to coordinate a group of people towards a goal. "I'm going to find out if they have a mop so that we can clean this up."

Administrator-Administrator
Wants to coordinate a group of people to coordinate a

group of people towards a goal. "Susan, get the waitress. Jim, pick up the glass. Ted, grab some napkins."

Administrator-Exhorter
Wants to encourage people about the future to coordinate a group of people towards a goal. "This will be fun to clean up together!"

FAMOUS EXAMPLES OF ADMINISTRATOR-WHYS

Administrator-Perceiver: General Patton (*Patton*), Chip Kelly (college football coach)
Administrator-Teacher: Willy Wonka, Glenn Frey (musician), Abe Lincoln, Morpheus (*The Matrix*)
Administrator-Compassion: Rick Rubin (music producer)
Administrator-Giver: The Giving Tree (children's book)
Administrator-Server: Benny "the Jet" Rodriguez (*The Sandlot*), Captain America, Dalton (*Road House*), The Wolf (*Pulp Fiction*), Magic Johnson (NBA player)
Administrator-Administrator: Lisa Cuddy (TV Show *House M.D.*)
Administrator-Exhorter: President Donald Trump, Jimmy Johnson (NFL football coach)

CHAPTER 9

EXHORTER

"Next time we will eat at the counter, and this won't happen!"

IN THIS chapter, we're going to hear from an Exhorter. Exhorters love to be the source of passion, motivation, and encouragement and are very focused on the future. An Exhorter loves to make things awesome, to the extreme. As a Compassion, I love to interact with Exhorters because they're often quick to share what's going on, which helps me know exactly how to help them.

To learn about Exhorters, we're going to hear from my sister, Jennifer. Jennifer is an Exhorter-Teacher who is extremely passionate about moving people forward. Talking to Jennifer is like talking to someone who just wants to be your biggest fan because she'll tell you all of the reasons that you're awesome to get you moving towards the future. She is a very passionate person and wants people to be as passionate as she is about anything and everything.

Jennifer, what exciting information would you like to share with us?

GROWING UP

Hi! I'm Jennifer, and I'm very excited to share what it's like to be an Exhorter. It can be pretty easy to misunderstand, and it can be pretty tough to live! I feel like I'm always moving between so many emotions that by the end of the day, I feel like I've been on ten adventures. I love it!

I was an outgoing person as a child - talkative and friendly with a bubbly personality. I wanted others to be encouraged and to feel as excited about the future as I felt. I think others generally accepted and appreciated this characteristic about me. Still, there were the skeptics that would say I was too optimistic or had my head in the clouds. Some people made little jabs that they probably felt were cute, like calling me the relentless cheerleader.

Growing up, I loved sports. I played volleyball in middle school and high school. I was known as the team cheerleader. I was the first one to cheer when my teammates would *kill* the volleyball over the net. I would yell when they served and got an ace. I'd be the one saying, "Watch the next serve, girls," "We got this," or, "Let's go!"

I wasn't the best player on my team, but I can remember my coach saying she needed me on the court when we fell behind. She would put me in the game just to encourage my teammates with a lot of, "We got this!" When someone would miss the ball, I'd say, "Shake it off, you'll get the next one!" And more often than not, we'd come back and win! I felt so much energy being able to encourage my team!

But being an Exhorter isn't all fun and games because I also remember when I was little how much I hated going to bed earlier than my older brothers. They got to stay up late, why didn't I? So I'd throw massive tantrums screaming about how it wasn't fair that I had to go to bed before them. I wanted them to feel what I felt like any Exhorter would, but I did that by throwing a tantrum so that they would *feel* how unfair it was too.

To get me to bed, my parents and brothers ended up working together and putting me to bed as a team, singing songs with me and talking about my day, the entire family giving me all of their attention just to get me to go to sleep. Looking back, I'm embarrassed at what a little terror I was!

As I got older and started to reflect on all of the comments made about how I was overly excited and too optimistic, I began to wonder if I was being unrealistic. Being an Exhorter, I didn't just feel a *little* unrealistic. I felt like my entire future was crashing, and I would start to feel so much fear about what the future might look like that I would tailspin until my mom would hold me, comfort me, and assure me about how bright my future would be.

WHO AM I

Exhorters want to encourage others so that they can move forward in their life. We can feel frustrated when people don't feel what we feel. Just like a Giver is trying to *give* you something and a Perceiver is trying to *show* you something, an Exhorter is trying to help you *feel* something.

It's easy to think about Exhorters in terms of being a "bro" or a "hippie" because a lot of what they experience is the feeling of a situation. It's the vibe. Exhorters want to pass along a positive vibe to you to help you feel remarkable about a situation.

The challenge of being an Exhorter or interacting with

> EXHORTERS WANT TO ENCOURAGE OTHERS SO THAT THEY CAN MOVE FORWARD IN THEIR LIFE.

an Exhorter is that they already have those vibes, and they're trying to get *you* to have those vibes as well. So it isn't just that they want you to feel awesome about a situation. *They* want to feel awesome about a situation, and *then* they want to get *you* to feel awesome, too.

Just like Compassion feels double the emotions of others, Exhorters want to feel double their own emotions, and they can do that by getting you to feel it too.

For a lot of Exhorters, we want to do this process in one step. We try to feel +10 and then get you to feel +10 right away so that we can feel +20! The problem is most people aren't ready for a +10 in one step. If someone is having a bad day and I try to get them excited about my good day, I'm probably just going to make them mad because I'm not giving them a chance to deal with their own feelings first.

Exhorters are often confused with Compassionators. We can seem like we want to help people who are stuck in a hole get out of a hole, or bad situation, because we are so encouraging, but we get drained by people stuck in a hole. It surprises others that I don't enjoy talking to those people. People think, "Jennifer is so nice. I'm sure she'd love to help so-and-so!"

Compassionators get tons of energy helping people who are down and out to get out of the hole. Exhorters want to help people who are doing good and encourage them to reach the mountaintop.

When people want to grow and become more of who they were created to be, it's through the pain of growth. Going up a mountaintop can be challenging. The air gets thinner. The terrain gets rougher. These warriors are fighting the environment with a passion for reaching their full potential. I want to be right beside them like a sherpa helping a climber climb Mt. Everest. I want to encourage them to continue forward to the best and most rewarding future beyond their imagination!

CONFIRMATION QUESTIONS

Do you want people to feel what you are feeling? Do you get frustrated when others don't feel what you feel? Do you run forward really quickly? Do you often imagine the future? Do you quickly get into fear about the future?

Do you think you are an Exhorter? Who do you know that might be an Exhorter?

DIRECTION

Exhorters are focused on the future and, most of the time, feel like they are living in that future. That's why a question my close friends will ask me is, "How far into the future are you living right now?" I feel like I live every day like it's two years in the future. I logically know today is today, but everything I'm working towards and thinking about is for a point in time that is two years ahead, and I'm trying to get there as quickly as possible. This can feel like a burden because it makes it really hard to be in the present moment and enjoy the here and now.

For three years before I permanently moved to Wisconsin, I drove back and forth from Illinois almost every weekend. I'd get in the car, turn on my favorite music at the time and imagine what the weekend was going to be like when I got to my friend's house. Having a natural foot in the future allowed me to drive and imagine my weekend. Those drives gave me lots of energy, and I didn't have any issues with the long distance.

METHOD

As an Exhorter, I just want to talk! Once, my brothers and I went to Six Flags. We were running around riding the rides, and I was having a decent time, but nothing spectacular. One of my brothers asked me, "What are you thinking about?"

I said, "Nothing," because just running around on roller coasters was kind of boring to me. He started to ask me questions about life, and we began to share. We figured out how I would handle work, school, and all kinds of things that I was looking forward to in the future. I started to have fun once we started talking about my future life. I don't want to just do things. I want to *talk* about the future *while* we do things. It's the imagination that gives me the energy.

When I encourage others, I do it through speaking. I try to influence them to feel the feelings I am feeling. I don't *do* things for others naturally. I am not the first person who will jump out of my seat to lend a hand. I encourage those who are jumping up to lend a hand.

THE WHY EFFECT

Exhorter WHYs feel the future opportunity and want others to feel what they feel. They want others to feel excited and encouraged.

I love meeting with people, especially women who feel stuck and want to change and grow. It's in these meetings that I get to listen to women share about how their insecurities and decisions have caused them to make less progress in their lives than they hoped. I know how that feels, and I know they can become more than they are currently imagining.

I start to get excited when I think of their bright future, so I encourage them to every day feel the excitement I feel. If they don't get excited, I keep adjusting to get them excited. When they finally see that future and feel encouraged, I feel on top of the world!

I've had jobs where I had to operate as a Server ID. As a customer service representative at a call center, my job was to answer phone calls and give information to customers. It was busy and boring for me because it didn't involve encouraging people in any way, and no one was feeling what I was feeling. The job was a bad fit for who I was created to be.

I want people to walk away from an interaction with me feeling like I'm for them and feeling my desire for them to reach their full potential, and that can often start with simple steps.

A friend of mine was having a recent issue with a coworker. Every day my friend tried to come into work with a positive attitude and focus on enjoying her work, but one coworker brought a ton of pessimism. This woman was bringing my friend down. I encouraged my friend to ask her coworker a few specific questions when her coworker started to get negative. The next time I saw my friend, she shared that she had tried my advice, and it actually stopped her coworker from going down those negative paths. She was so excited that it worked, and that made me feel incredible!

THE HOW CONNECTION

Exhorter HOWs want to do the encouraging. You see them as the cheerleader, optimist, and motivational speaker. They typically bring energy to any situation and get everyone pumped up.

I have a coworker, Debra, who is an Exhorter HOW. She is well-known for walking into any meeting and getting the team excited to discuss the meeting topic. She will even bust out singing little jingles to loosen everyone up.

That is different from me as an Exhorter WHY. I will sit in the meeting and start to see the future vision for our team, and I begin to get excited. It isn't until after I start to get excited that I want everyone else to feel excited about that future. I will kick in and begin to energize the team until they're feeling what I'm feeling.

HOW TO HELP

There are some significant "Exhorter Rules" to help others learn how to talk to Exhorters for the Exhorter's benefit. This is hugely important because we have many feelings, and those feelings are very precious to us.

The first step is to let the Exhorter talk first. Exhorters feel many things and want to take things forward, so the first few minutes of any interaction can make or break it. If the non-Exhorter talks for the first fifteen minutes and then the Exhorter talks for an hour, the Exhorter will feel like the non-Exhorter did all the talking. If the Exhorter talks and shares for the first fifteen minutes, and then the non-Exhorter talks for an hour, the Exhorter will feel like they did all the talking and the non-Exhorter just listened to them.

The second step is to feel what they feel; mirror their emotions. The easiest way to do this is to make the same facial expression. Ideally, you would feel what they are feeling, but if you aren't, determine something that makes you feel the same way as they feel and respond with that! Remember, the Exhorter is much more focused on the emotion than the facts. If you can't do that, then at least acknowledge their feelings. This is an excellent lesson to learn when interacting with anybody, but it will be the deciding factor for how the interaction is remembered for an Exhorter.

A friend was sharing about interacting with his wife, an Exhorter. He shared that no matter what happens when they get in an argument, she feels like he doesn't understand what she is saying. He had literally written down her argument and stated it back to her, and she responded by saying he still didn't understand.

Once he learned to focus first on *feeling* what she *felt*, the next time they had an argument, he repeated what she was saying with the same feeling and said he understood her. He took this even further and tried stating the wrong information with the right feelings. She still felt like he understood her.

Finally, remember that Exhorters want to get people on top of a mountain, not pull people out of a hole. If you have a problem where you need an Exhorter's help, present the problem as trying to get something on top of a mountain. Try to share your objective with the Exhorter, the awesome place where you want to be, and then tell them what's in the way. The Exhorter should respond well.

If you approach the Exhorter telling them how bad a situation is and ask for help, then they are going to feel instantly drained, and, instead of wanting to help you get the problem fixed, they'll feel like you're the problem because you're so focused on negative things. One way to approach this is to tell the Exhorter you want to make a situation better and then ask them for help. If you start with how you are looking to improve something, they feel like you both are on the same page.

MISUNDERSTOOD

Remember, an Exhorter wants you to feel what they feel. It can be when they are excited about the future, as well as when they're feeling bummed out or angry. They want you to feel that, too. This can make Exhorters appear to be narcissists, but the quickest way to reach them is to feel what they feel.

Exhorters can also be seen as liars or exaggerators. Remember, the Exhorter is focused on you feeling what they are feeling. If their first presentation of the issue doesn't get the desired emotion, the Exhorter may exaggerate the facts to get you to feel the emotion. If that doesn't work, they can state something that isn't a fact. The Exhorter's intent is not to mislead you by exaggerating or lying. They intend to get you to feel what they feel, so changing these facts is an effect of trying to get the response their uniqueness craves.

Unfortunately, many Exhorters don't want to slow down or ever feel like they're not going to get where they want to go quickly enough, and they end up crashing from their high points. For a lot of Exhorters, they spend their lives in this process. They'll try to get as far forward as they can, then they'll start to feel bad about something, and they'll run away from that feeling because feeling bad isn't encouraging. How do they do that, and what does it look like to the rest of us? The Exhorter will say things are twice as good as they really are.

Typically, if someone asks me how I'm doing, I'll respond with, "I'm doing great!" If I'm starting to feel bad, and I'm not feeling confident in myself, when they ask me how I'm doing, I'll respond with even *more* positive statements such as, "I'm feeling amazing! I've never felt better! Isn't it the greatest thing just to be alive?"

From the outside, this can look like I'm manic. A few days later, when I can't keep up the charade, I crash and fall into despair. When an Exhorter crashes, there is no emotion left. They just feel nothing.

> **MOST EXHORTERS DON'T NATURALLY HAVE A GOOD SENSE FOR WHEN THEY ARE BEING FUN OR NOT.**

This causes Exhorters who try to be their Intangible Driver in one step to appear bipolar. When we start to feel bad, we instead act like we're better than we've ever been (manic), and then we suddenly crash soon after and have no energy for anything (depressive).

To everyone, it looks like the Exhorter went from the mountaintop to the bottom of a pit. However, what appeared to be a mountaintop experience was really them sliding into the pit and trying to exhort themselves out of the pit. Not only does this look bipolar, but this whipsawing of the Exhorter's body chemistry can also throw it out of whack.

Exhorter bosses appear to be bipolar because of the third step of the "Exhorter Rules" mentioned above. When you tell the Exhorter boss that someone is preventing you from accomplishing your job, the Exhorter boss is being put in a hole, and they will respond with something like, "Why don't you come to me with solutions instead of problems?"

However, if you tell the Exhorter boss you are trying to accomplish something, but you are having a tough time, the Exhorter boss will now ask you what's wrong to exhort you! When you tell the boss the "someone" who is preventing you from accomplishing your job, the Exhorter boss will confront that person. When people tell me their boss sometimes screams at them and sometimes will do anything for them, I know they are an Exhorter, and the reason for their bipolar appearance is how the employee approaches them.

An Exhorter needs to learn how to slow down and make progress in *healthy ways*. It can sound like the worst thing in the world to an Exhorter, but by slowing down, we can find the right way to move forward. Even more, it will let us go forward at the speed that leads us to the positive future we so desire.

Another issue common for Exhorters is they don't have a great sense of reality. They are focused on feelings, which may not line up with reality, *and* they want to help you have a good time. The result is Exhorters *feel* like they are a fun person and that everything they say or do is fun, even if it isn't.

I had a friend who was quitting a job due to stress, and his Exhorter boss kept making jokes about him retiring. He was 30. My friend knew that the boss wasn't trying to offend him and realized the boss thought he was funny, but it wasn't. The boss didn't know how to handle that situation, and my friend wound up feeling frustrated because it felt like his stress was being laughed off.

Most Exhorters don't naturally have a good sense for when they are being fun or not. Many Exhorters grow up with no one feeling what they feel, so they have a tough time telling if something is actually fun. If they start making a joke or playing around and someone tells them to stop, they aren't totally sure if the person actually wants them to stop or if they're just playing along.

Deb has two kids, Pete, a nine-year-old, and Davey, a six-year-old Exhorter that struggles with this inability to determine if others are having fun or not. Pete will be playing with some toys, and Davey will sit down next to him and start grabbing the toys. Pete laughs and says, stop it, so Davey thinks his brother is having fun. He *did* laugh, so Davey keeps going. Then his brother says stop it in a more serious voice. Davey isn't sure if the serious voice is real or if his brother is still playing along. He *did* start by laughing, after all.

So Davey keeps going. His brother responds by pushing him down and yelling at him, saying that Davey is always ruining his fun. Now Pete feels bad, and Davey suddenly goes from feeling like they're having fun to feeling like they're fighting, and he gets mad. What started as two brothers having fun together quickly turns into a sibling brawl. Afterward, Davey doesn't understand what happened, and he feels very emotional. To him, he was just trying to help his brother have fun, and his brother responded by getting mad.

Deb has started to help Davey focus on trying to help his brother have fun for Pete's benefit, and she has begun to help Pete communicate with his Exhorter brother. Now, Davey is learning to help his brother have fun instead of just trying to have fun for himself. Pete is learning to share his thoughts, such as, "This isn't fun," instead of just trying to shout, "Stop it!"

The brothers are starting to build a healthier relationship because of that communication, and Deb is experiencing a lot less stress at home.

Exhorters tend to grow up learning through experience when something is actually fun and when it isn't, and often they still struggle to tell even as they grow older. That's why Exhorters can seem so difficult before the age of 25. It takes 25 years to learn through experience when things are fun and when they are not fun.

As an Exhorter, I have learned to appreciate people who will let me know directly when I am being pushy and obnoxious and that something is *not* fun to them. I will immediately stop, often thanking them for letting me know. Likewise, I also appreciate it when people tell me when they find something I am doing to be fun.

UNHEALTHY USE OF ID

Exhorters tend to get off track by using their very powerful imagination. Remember, Exhorters are usually living their lives like it is months or years in the future. This means they have a plan that would result in them getting where they want to be, and when something doesn't go the right way, it can feel like their *entire future* is at stake. This causes them to feel fear. Exhorters can get into fear because of their ability to imagine.

For example, while traveling through the desert, some people might think they could get bitten by a snake. This isn't fear but rather a rational concern. Fear is a couple of steps further. An Exhorter might realize that they could get bitten by a snake and then get into fear by thinking, "What if I got bit by a snake and didn't even know it?" That thought is followed very quickly by, "What if a snake already bit me, and I'm already going to die, and it's already too late, and I never even got a chance to get married or have kids and, and, and…?"

That's Exhorter fear. No matter what I do, my life might already be ruined because I can imagine the worst, future case scenarios.

Exhorters should try to use their imagination in more healthy ways by thinking about all of the other things that could happen as the first step, rather than all the things that could occur *after* the first step.

So, instead of imagining how a snake could have already bitten them, they could imagine what *else* could happen while driving through the desert.

"I could get bit by a snake."
"I could see a cactus up close and in person!"
"I could see a sunset over the desert; that would be pretty!"
"My car could break down!"

Once they've imagined many options, they can then think of how they would respond to each one separately. That way, they feel like they always have another option and a way to handle the situation. They aren't powerless.

Many Exhorters struggle to learn this skill because it can be scary to think of bad things happening, but bad things will happen. It is inevitable, but we can always respond to bad things well.

I went on a road trip to Michigan with my boyfriend. We were going to celebrate finishing a project we worked on together. On the way there, about three hours into a six-hour road trip, I was driving, and my boyfriend took a nap. I had a few minutes alone with my thoughts, and I started to run forward with my imagination, thinking that he wasn't having a good time because he was sleeping. But we were there to celebrate all the hard work we've done. If he's sleeping, that means all the work we've done in the past isn't important to him, and when we get back from the trip I'm going to have to tell everyone that the trip was awful and it wasn't fun!

My thoughts were racing!

When he woke up, I thought I was going to have a panic attack, but I shared all of my feelings with him. At first, it was tense because I felt like something was wrong, but after we talked it out, he helped me see that I had just run forward with my imagination, and all of my worries were just in my head. He helped me pull back to reality, which can be a huge challenge! We ended up having great conversations and enjoyed our time together. The trip was a huge success, and we had a lot of fun! I'm glad he helped me get back in the moment.

RELATIONSHIPS

Exhorters tend to be attracted to Compassion because Compassion *wants* to feel what others are feeling. Unfortunately, if the Exhorter is not excellent enough to let the Compassion share as well, then the relationship tends to fizzle over time.

Many friendships and marriages go through this cycle. At first, there is a lot of energy because the Exhorter gets to share, and the

Compassion gets to care. However, over time the Compassion feels their own pain, and sometimes the Exhorter doesn't give them a chance to share. That Compassion will explode at some point, getting their pain out and potentially ruining the relationship. Exhorters definitely feel un-exhorted when someone explodes and is upset.

Exhorters need to learn to take that backward step and show compassion to others to keep the relationship balanced, or they'll end up taking advantage of the Compassion person without realizing it.

Exhorters tend to avoid Perceivers because Perceivers can sound negative. When Exhorters take the ice cream quiz and hear the Perceiver response of, "You dropped your sundae," they will often make a disgusted face and might even say, "No one would say that!"

I have a Perceiver friend who has an Exhorter boss, and their relationship can be complicated for both of them. The Perceiver sees all of the areas that the organization needs to work on so that business can grow but can't just say that directly to her boss because the boss will only see her as negative. Instead, if she wants to make him aware of an issue, she has to start her sentence by saying, "This organization could be awesome if we just…" When she focuses on how the place could be great, he doesn't hear that something is wrong, he hears that they are going to make something better.

Exhorters want to help situations be more fun and more enjoyable, so they are naturally attracted to people who are good at improvisation and approach situations with a positive attitude. For the same reasons, Exhorters struggle to interact with people who seem bummed out and mopey all of the time. An Exhorter might try to help someone who is bummed out have a good time, and when that person responds by complaining more, the Exhorter is quickly turned off and moves on.

CAREERS

Exhorters often end up getting into careers that involve motivational speaking. Talented public figures are often Exhorters because they can get a crowd to feel what they feel about a topic, and people usually vote based on a feeling.

Artists are often Exhorters. Notice when you talk to an artist, it's all about how they feel. Their art is an expression of *their* feelings.

CEOs and upper-level management are often Exhorters because they can be visionaries and see where the organization could go and what it can be. They can often inspire the employees to work towards the mountaintop.

CHILDREN: PARENTING AND TEACHING

Exhorters who had a parent or friends growing up who would feel what they felt usually end up being well-adjusted. However, many Exhorters grow up feeling misunderstood most of the time because others won't or don't feel what they feel. A simple example is when I was a kid and I would feel excited about a kids movie, but my parents didn't feel excited about the film. Just like that, I felt misunderstood.

This can cause Exhorters to feel a lot of frustration when they're growing up, and they often learn to vent that frustration in destructive ways. Have you ever experienced a kid who intentionally does something to upset you? I was doing this when I started screaming at my family because I had to go to bed before my brothers. It was my one sure-fire way to get others to feel what I felt. It was as if I was thinking, "If I'm frustrated or angry, I can make you frustrated and angry in *one* step." Remember, an Exhorter is trying to move forward as quickly as possible.

If an Exhorter child gets angry or frustrated and doesn't have someone in their life who will feel that way with them, they're likely to learn that destroying something, especially something someone else cares about, will cause someone else to feel that too. Many of these children end up in the Emotional and Behavioral Disorders (EBD) system in school because the only coping mechanism is to act destructively.

For teachers who specialize in working with students with emotional and behavioral disorders, their training will often encourage them to avoid giving agency or validity to a student's negative feelings. They are trained not to relate to the student's feelings because the child might think that negative emotion is okay. They are trained to respond respectfully and calmly instead.

Unfortunately, many of the kids who have emotional and behavioral disorders are Exhorters. Because these trained adults aren't willing to feel what the child is feeling first, Exhorters spend most of their youth feeling misunderstood. When an Exhorter is in an Emotional/Behavioral Disorder (EBD) classroom and gets angry, the teacher is trained not to feel what they feel, which will actually cause an Exhorter to get even more upset!

When EBD teachers are taught to respond to Exhorters by feeling what the student feels first, even if the fact or context isn't reality, it completely turns the situation into a positive outcome. You can feel what an Exhorter is feeling without agreeing with their perspective on reality.

One teacher shared how when she was trying to get the students to sit in a circle to start a lesson, one Exhorter was having a rough morning and started getting angry. He stood up on a desk and started shouting his feelings at the teacher. He was feeling angry. The teacher responded by stating firmly, "I also feel angry when students don't participate in our learning time!" The student instantly got down from the desk and took his seat. If you want to reach an Exhorter, let your first step be to feel what they feel.

Remember, Exhorters can exaggerate or appear to lie to get you to feel what they feel, especially if it is to get themselves exhorted. One of the key techniques to teach an Exhorter child is how they feel the most exhorted when they help others feel encouraged about their own lives.

SELF HELP

One of the greatest lessons an Exhorter can learn is to be more compassionate as a first step and then lead the person one feeling at a time towards being exhorted. Ultimately, a healthy Exhorter wants you to feel how much they care.

A friend of mine was helping a Server-Server mom with her two sons, Kyle and Devon. Devon is an Exhorter, and Kyle is a Compassion. Every day, Kyle would feel drained because Devon was trying to get him excited about what Devon felt excited about. Devon was throwing himself a party every day, and it was wearing Kyle down.

Exhorters are trying to throw a party, and the easiest way to throw a party every day is to throw one for themselves, but they have to convince everyone else to focus on them, which comes across as selfish.

So my friend suggested to the mother to ask Devon, "How would you like to be at a party every day? The way to do that is to throw a party for *someone else* every day. Then you will always be at a party." Devon was so excited about the suggestion! Exhorters care more about being at the party than about the party being for them. They just want to *feel* the party!

When Exhorters finally learn how to throw a party for others, people start to feel like the Exhorter is very caring, instead of feeling like the Exhorter is a narcissist. Mature Exhorters are experts at helping people feel how much they care about them.

CHEAT SHEET

Exhorter-Perceiver
Wants to make people aware of an issue to encourage them about the future. "Next time, we will go to a better ice cream shop."

Exhorter-Teacher
Wants to help people understand why an issue exists to encourage them about the future. "This won't happen next time because we will sit at the counter."

Exhorter-Compassion
Wants to bear the emotional pain of people to encourage them about the future. "Don't get upset. We're going to look back at this and laugh."

Exhorter-Giver
Wants to give a tangible gift or improvement to people to encourage them about the future. "Let me buy you a bigger sundae."

Exhorter-Server
Wants to fill a need to encourage people about the future. "I will clean this up. Sit down and relax."

> The most energetic and accomplished people in business tend to be Exhorter-Server. They will do whatever it takes to get others to feel excited. These people are not only instantly likable, but they are also fun to hang around!

The downside is that while everyone else "doubles down" when they encounter an obstacle, I like to say Exhorters "triple down," and no one is better at doing this than Exhorter-Server. Notice, they can do whatever it takes (Server HOW) to put themselves infinitely in the future (Exhorter WHY.) This means they hate to talk about the past, and they are especially un-exhorted by talking about their mistakes and failures. If they do talk about the past, it is only to prove how they can't be stopped in the future.

Yes, there are many Exhorter-Servers seen as inspirational figures. However, if they don't know how to anchor themselves in reality, the end of their story can become anything other than encouraging.

Exhorter-Administrator
Wants to coordinate a group of people to encourage people about the future. "Ted and Marcia will clean this up while I talk to the manager. Sit down and relax."

Exhorter-Exhorter
Wants to encourage people about the future to encourage them about the future. "This will be fun to clean up."

FAMOUS EXAMPLES OF EXHORTER-WHYS

Exhorter-Perceiver: Yoda (*Star Wars*), Steve Jobs (Co-Founder of Apple), Taylor Swift (musician)
Exhorter-Teacher: Michael Squints (*The Sandlot*),

Vince Vaughn (actor), Tony Robbins (motivational coach)

Exhorter-Compassion: Phil Dunphy (TV show *Modern Family*), Michael Scott (TV show *The Office*)

Exhorter-Giver: Ellen Degeneres (comedian), Barney (Children's TV dinosaur character)

Exhorter-Server: Oprah (talk show host), The Flash, Iron Man, Lance Armstrong (cyclist),

Exhorter-Administrator: Pete Carrol (NFL coach)

Exhorter-Exhorter: Hype man (rapper), Ray Lewis (NFL football player)

CHAPTER 10

DETERMINING THE UNIQUENESS OF OTHERS

PAST
↓
Perceiver
↓
Teacher
↓
Compassion
↓
Giver
↓
Server
↓
Administrator
↓
Exhorter
↓
FUTURE

NOW THAT you have a good understanding of your uniqueness and the uniqueness of others, this section of the book is meant to help you with practical applications when it comes to diagnosing and helping others and improving your relationships. Let's begin by trying to determine the uniqueness of others.

It helps if we use the box on the left to see how we go from Past to Future-focused:

Two groups jump out: Past-Past and Future-Future.

A Past-Past person is any WHY-HOW combination that is only made up of Perceiver, Teacher, and/or Compassion. These individuals will focus on the past and lose energy when you try to talk about the future. Questions like "What are you going to do tomorrow?"

or "Where do you see yourself in five years?" completely drain these people. They will tend to talk in past tenses.

A Future-Future person is any WHY-HOW combination that is only made up of Server, Administrator, and/or Exhorter. These individuals will focus on the future and lose energy when you try to talk about the past. Questions like "What did you do yesterday?" or "What was your childhood like?" completely drain these people. They will tend to talk in future tenses.

For example, an elementary student got sent out of her room for disciplinary reasons. When she was asked what she did, she completely ignored the question. An educator trained in the Intangible Driver information recognized the student as Future-Future and asked the student, "If I ask your teacher what you did, what would she say?" The student immediately said, "She would tell you I asked to go to the bathroom, and when she said no, I left the class." Notice, both halves of the question were phrased in the future tense, and the student turned out to be Exhorter-Administrator.

Once you identify a person as fitting in either of these groups, you have the possible IDs narrowed to three. Pick a combination and begin interacting with them according to that option and see if they gain or lose energy. Depending on how much energy they gain or lose, you will be able to tell how close you are to being right.

If the person doesn't fit into one of these two groups, this leads to another diagnostic tool to help determine their uniqueness.

MISUNDERSTOOD

The nature of feeling misunderstood depends on the distance between the WHY and HOW position of your Intangible Driver. The further the distance, the more often the person feels misunderstood. The shorter the distance, the less a person feels misunderstood.

Those whose WHY and HOW are the same, such as Exhorter-Exhorter or Teacher-Teacher, are the least misunderstood. An Exhorter-Exhorter wants others to be Exhorted, and they connect with others by Exhorting. There is very little to confuse. They are Exhorters. People will say about these people, "They are who they are," because they don't appear to change over time.

Notice, people who are Past-Past or Future-Future have very little difference between their WHY and HOW, so they tend not to appear to change over time.

On the other hand, Perceiver-Exhorters and Exhorter-Perceivers have the most significant distance between their WHY and HOW and are often misunderstood. Are they trying to help others see the past, or are they wanting others to be encouraged about the future? Are they focused on facts to the exclusion of feelings or focused on feelings to the exclusion of facts? That's a big difference. These people appear to change over time. The direction of the change between these two groups is very different.

For example, my colleague, John, and I often work together as executive coaches. I'm a Compassion-Server, and John is an Administrator-Teacher. There are two units between my Compassion WHY and Server HOW. John has four units in between his Administrator WHY and Teacher HOW.

Our clients have always felt like I'm a nice guy when they first meet me. Upfront, I am looking to connect with them by finding the need and filling it. As people get to know me, they don't believe I change that much. It's not a big jump for them between my Server and my Compassion. However, the slight difference they do notice is I'm more serious than what they had initially thought. I'm not the future-focused Server. I am the past-focused Compassion person wondering what happened.

When they first meet John, he connects with them by teaching. He sounds like a scientist, explaining a new concept from neurochemistry or psychology. Even though he's a good Teacher and many of his points are shared through stories, people still feel like they are attending a college lecture.

As people get to know John, they see more and more of the Administrator, and they start to realize that is his WHY. He cares about the group dynamic *more* than the individuals in the group. He likes to move people around in a group to get the best result, and it can feel like he's trying to play a game. This relatively significant difference between his HOW and WHY results in people thinking that he has changed over time. Since John hasn't changed, he feels misunderstood.

Notice, John appears to become more fun as you get to know him, making him feel justified in previously feeling misunderstood. He sees himself as the future-focused Administrator, while everyone initially reacts to him like he's the lecturing Teacher.

My rule of thumb is: if the person appears to change between the first time you meet them and the fourth time you meet them, they have a difference of at least four units between their WHY and HOW.

When I help people who are struggling to interact with someone, this is one of the first areas I explore. Did you misunderstand the person? Does the person misunderstand you? Either way, identifying

> WHEN I HELP PEOPLE WHO ARE STRUGGLING TO INTERACT WITH SOMEONE, THIS IS ONE OF THE FIRST AREAS I EXPLORE.

the gap in the IDs can help bring understanding to what is motivating the individual.

Finally, if none of this helps the person's ID to become readily apparent, consider Giver. Since Giver is in the present, it can act as a wild card, meaning it can mirror the direction of the other ID. Giver-Server can appear Future-Future, while Perceiver-Giver can appear Past-Past. The issue is, they won't speak only about the Future or the Past, respectively.

USE YOURSELF

The best way to determine the uniqueness of others is to know and have confidence in your own uniqueness!

For example, if you are Small Picture, it is readily apparent who you interact with that is Small Picture and who is Big Picture. The Small Picture IDs are the ones you immediately feel comfortable with, while the Big Picture IDs feel different.

Likewise, if you are an External Processor, you can tell the other External Processors because they tend to be just as open with what they are thinking as you.

Notice, once you know your uniqueness, the measure for the uniqueness of others is tension. This is especially true when it comes to their ID.

TENSION

Imagine what it would be like for a Perceiver-Perceiver, someone focused on pointing out the facts regardless of the feelings, to interact with an Exhorter-Exhorter, someone focused on the feeling of the situation with an unending optimism, regardless of the facts. Do you think there would be tension between the two? Do you think it could be an awkward interaction? It could be! Why?

The distance between two individual's WHYs directly relates to how much tension they experience with each other. In contrast, the closeness between our HOWs directly relates to how easily we can make a connection.

Remember Simon and Jennifer? Simon is a Perceiver WHY, and Jennifer is an Exhorter WHY. When they interact, they almost always want to take the situation in opposite directions. Simon wants people to be aware of a fact, and he can seem negative. Jennifer wants people to feel excited, so they can have the courage to move forward into the future.

Wouldn't it be great if we could have both of those things happen? Of course! However, both of them will feel like we're taking a backward step further away from their objective every time the other person takes a forward step. Each step towards dealing with the fact feels less like things are going forward for Jennifer, and each step towards having the courage to move into the future feels like things are less grounded in reality to Simon.

It's as if my car broke down, completely died, and I was hanging out with Simon and Jennifer. They'll both approach me differently. Simon would say, "This car is a pile of junk." Jennifer would say, "Just think of how amazing your next car is going to be! We could start shopping for the car of your dreams!"

Do you feel the whiplash? Facts, future, facts, future. We're going back and forth. Jennifer and Simon would experience a lot of tension as they both try to help me.

When we talk about the tension individuals experience as an effect of their Intangible Drivers, we grade it on a 0-6 scale. We would give a 0 to two people who have the same WHY and a 6 to the people who have the farthest WHYs from each other. A Perceiver interacting with an Exhorter would be a 6 tension level. If someone is a Compassion, then the most tension they could experience would be interacting with an Exhorter, which is 4 steps away on the spectrum.

In the example of my car breaking down, I'm a Compassion WHY, so I feel less tension talking to Simon. Simon perceiving is only two steps away from my Compassion, so it's not that hard to get there. But Jennifer talking about the next car I'm going to have is tougher to relate to because Exhorter is four steps away.

If my wife, Morgan, was in the same situation as a Server WHY she would already be a few days in the future thinking about where she'll have to go to find a new car. She might already be thinking about which dealership she's going to visit. She would experience a lot less tension with Jennifer because she's already thinking forward. Simon pointing out the facts would feel like he's pulling her back into the past, looking at the broken car instead of thinking about how to get a new one. Exhorter is two steps away from Server, while Perceiver is four steps away from Server.

CONNECTION

We experience a connection when our HOW interacts with another person's HOW. This feeling of connection is called a release. When our WHYs are interacting with others, we feel the tension. When our HOWs connect, that tension is released. That tension being released is the proof of the connection.

When two individuals have the same HOW, it's an easier connection. Suppose two people do not have the same HOW. One of the individuals will have to adjust for a connection to occur.

Back to our Perceiver-Perceiver with an Exhorter-Exhorter example. These two individuals would have the most tension possible *and* the most difficult time connecting. It would be an extremely tense and awkward interaction. We tend to feel awkward around people when we struggle to connect.

If an Exhorter-Teacher interacted with a Compassion-Teacher, they could experience a significant amount of tension because their WHYs are further apart. Still, they'd have a very easy time releasing the tension once they connected through their Teacher HOWs. They could have a lot of fun teaching each other and learning from each other. That means those two would have interactions that were both deep *and* enjoyable.

This is an incredibly useful tool! I especially enjoy helping couples, dating or married, resolve issues that typically come up because one or both of the individuals refuse to adjust their HOW.

I can usually tell how a relationship will go when the couple starts dating based on their Intangible Drivers. For example, two Exhorter WHYs won't experience much tension. They will immediately get along, like two Internal Processors or two Big Picture people. However, it will be hard to have profound and memorable experiences together because the tension never builds. Having similar WHYs is like riding the kiddie train at an amusement park. It can be fun in the short term, but there is really no tension and, therefore, no big release.

If our WHYs are far apart, it's like riding the fast and furious rollercoaster. The tension builds and builds and builds, and then BAM… a huge release when they connect in their HOWs! The more tension in their WHYs, the bigger the potential release in the HOWs. However, there will be an initial discomfort that needs to be overcome, like an Internal Processor with an External Processor or a Big Picture person with a Small Picture person.

Let's look at how to use this information to diagnose relationships in the next chapter.

CHAPTER 11

HEALTHY RELATIONSHIPS

IN THE previous chapter, we learned a tool for diagnosing the uniqueness of others and found how the best way to determine the uniqueness of others begins by knowing and being confident of our own uniqueness.

With all of that said, let's apply this to your relationships, especially the ones you have with your spouse, close friends or relatives, and your role model, such as a parent or someone who influenced your life.

Often, those with who we are closest are the ones with whom we have the most tension. The issue is the connection. When we don't get the tension relieved when interacting with someone, we tend to feel awkward and frustrated. Think of individuals that you feel awkward around or struggle to interact with and you might realize you don't connect with their HOW.

We can break these relationships down into three types:
- Two non-Server HOWs
- One Server HOW and one non-Server HOW
- Two Server HOWs

Let's get into the nitty-gritty on each one.

TWO NON-SERVER HOWS

When two non-Server HOWs interact, the connection is hit or miss. Either their HOWs line up and they get along, or they don't. I've noticed that people tend to gravitate towards each other based on their HOWs. However, people who don't have the same HOW can still get along, but it requires one of them to adjust. For a non-Server, this isn't *natural* to do, and they need to simply understand that they won't get as much energy as if they could stay and connect in their HOW.

If a Compassion-Perceiver is interacting with a Teacher-Teacher, one of them will need to adjust to feel connected. Perceiver and Teacher aren't very far apart, so it isn't a big adjustment for either of them to make.

For a Compassion-Perceiver to interact with a Perceiver-Exhorter, the connection will take more effort by one of them to move further on the spectrum to meet up. If one of them does not adjust to the other's HOW, they might struggle to connect and understand each other. The Compassion-Perceiver would feel like the Perceiver-Exhorter is not aware, and Perceiver-Exhorter would feel like the Compassion-Perceiver is not encouraged about the future. That is a hard adjustment for both of these IDs, but for them to get along, someone is going to have to adjust.

Think back to parents or teachers dealing with two children who don't get along. They would say, "Why don't you take turns? Do it her way this time, and then she'll do it your way next time."

For relationships like this to be successful long-term, it usually requires each person to adjust 50% of the time. If that's too much for either person, then the relationship is going to struggle. If one of the individuals is unwilling to adjust, the other will eventually lose all their energy.

ONE SERVER HOW & ONE NON-SERVER HOW

In a relationship that includes a Server and a non-Server, this dynamic shifts. That's because Servers get energy from adjusting, *and* they do it naturally. Again, this causes others to think Servers are good people and that everyone else isn't as flexible. However, there are challenges.

Imagine a quarterback is a Server. They play an away game in a different city, and the crowd wants them to lose. The fans boo the Server quarterback every time they are on the field. What does the Server do in response? Naturally, they want to adjust to the crowd. So they start playing worse and cause their team to make mistakes. Worse, there are ten other teammates in their immediate vicinity. All it takes is one of these ten players to be upset, and the quarterback will naturally adjust to them and become upset as well!

The best quarterbacks in the NFL are non-Servers. They are the ones who get everyone on the team to adjust to them regardless of the crowd. The same can be said of executives. Often, when the company leaders are Servers, they tend to try to adjust to everyone in the company, including low-performing team members, and hurt the business's longevity. I've known executives who work around this issue by *avoiding* interactions with low-performing team members because they know they will struggle to not adjust to them.

Marty, a Compassion-Server, is a plant manager who struggles to say "no" to anyone who wants time off, even if it means he has to work extra hours that week to ensure all the work gets done. He loses energy during confrontations, so he avoids them by adjusting in the moment to the person wanting time off.

When it comes to relationships, the Server/Non-Server relationships usually result in the most dramatic aha moments. A woman took the ID quiz and discovered she is Server-Giver. She immediately wanted to know her husband's ID. When the tester asked what she thought he was, she said, "I think he's a Giver, but a different type of Giver than me." Right there, the tester knew he was Server and was moving to Giver to avoid fights.

The husband was given the quiz, and he is Teacher-Server. The tester told the couple that every time they get along, the husband moves to Giver, and every time they fight, it is because the husband doesn't move to Giver.

The couple had been married less than five years, and the husband's eyes widened as he said, "How can you know that? Are you looking into our windows?"

This response occurs because the couple's disagreements seem to be random. However, when this information is applied, all of the couple's interactions instantly divide into two groupings: agreements and disagreements. The factor is whether the Server HOW moves to meet the non-Server HOW.

When the wife realized the accuracy of this explanation, she became sad and said, "So, I'm making him have to move to me?" Again, she was reminded that Server HOW *likes* to move in response to a need.

TWO SERVER HOWS

Finally, the last combination is two Server HOWs. One would think this would be perfect and a match made in heaven that requires no effort, but that isn't the case. Because Servers adjust to the need that they see, two Server HOWs can (and often do) end up disagreeing on the need.

As I've shared, I'm Compassion-Server, and my wife, Morgan, is Server-Server.

A friend of ours crashed his car and needed help. I noticed that he was parked in a neighbor's driveway, and the vehicle was leaking antifreeze. That wouldn't have been a big deal for me except that the neighbor had a dog, dogs like the taste of antifreeze because it's sweet, but it's toxic and I didn't want to kill the neighbor's dog! I said we needed to take care of the spill. On the other hand, Morgan was focused on the coordination of people related to the crashed car. How was the car owner going to get to where he needed to go and the other people affected by the crashed car? We started to argue about what we both saw as the most significant need and tried to convince the other person we were right!

Notice, there are only seven possible needs! When Server HOW couples learn this information, they can avoid disagreements by simply asking each other, "What do you see as the need?" knowing it has to be one of seven answers.

The success of two Server HOW marriages and relationships is dependent on the quality and frequency of their communication. Increased communication with two Server HOWs make it more likely they will understand each other's perspective on the need.

This is also why two Server HOWs tend to be wary the first time they meet. For example, when two Teacher HOWs meet for the first time, they will talk like they've known each other for years. They just click. However, two Server HOWs are constantly trying to figure out the other person, making them a moving target to the other person who is themselves a moving target. It can be like watching two dogs circle each other for a few minutes before they start playing.

INTERNAL TENSION

The difference in a person's WHY and HOW creates internal tension. This is another way to guide you in determining the ID of another person! This attribute shows up in two ways.

First, people will only share deeply once the external tension is less than their internal tension. This means people with little to no internal tension, such as Perceiver-Perceiver, tend to avoid sharing deeply about themselves. Notice, this doesn't mean they won't talk a lot. It just means, if you listen carefully, they won't talk about themselves in a way that shares what they are deeply feeling.

> PEOPLE WHO HAVE LITTLE TO NO INTERNAL TENSION ARE EASILY INTIMIDATED BY EXTERNAL TENSION.

On the other hand, people with a lot of internal tension, such as Exhorter-Teacher are the ones who tend to share too much personal information about themselves. This leads to the second attribute.

People who have little to no internal tension are easily intimidated by external tension. They can be silenced by situations that contain a high amount of tension. Notice, the IDs that the general population see as "good" (Compassion, Giver, and Server) are in the middle of the tension spectrum. Not only are these IDs unable to have the greatest amount of internal tension, when they have both of these, but they are also easily intimidated. The most internal tension a person can have if they have both of these is 2 units (Compassion-Server or Server-Compassion). It doesn't take much external tension to exceed 2 units, and these people will quickly feel unsafe and comply in the short-term to avoid the tense situation.

Because they get so much energy helping others, they don't get energy being helped. This combination causes them to not ask for help when they are beginning to experience issues, even refusing offers of help by saying, "I'm fine." Then, when the tension is overwhelming, they suddenly break down as if the last straw was entirely responsible for their meltdown. However, when they are asked when they began to have a problem, you find out it had been for quite some time.

People who have significant amounts of internal tension are hard to intimidate. If you try to bring external tension, they are likely to bring all their internal tension out. There was a middle school teacher who was very muscular and controlled his class through intimidation. However, he quit halfway through the year because no matter what he did, the classroom ended up in shambles because of three students! What were their IDs? Exhorter-Perceiver, Administrator-Perceiver, and Exhorter-Teacher. The teacher was Giver-Perceiver. He had three units of internal tension, and it was no match for the students.

ADJUSTING TO PERSPECTIVES

The difference in picture perspective is a source of tension between people, and if we know how to use it intentionally, we can handle that tension well.

When a Big Picture person starts talking to a Small Picture person, it can feel like they are unloading a lot of information because they make larger jumps between facts than the Small Picture person would typically make. It can quickly feel overwhelming because the Small Picture person feels like they must remember everything they are told to participate in the interaction.

Likewise, when a Small Picture person starts talking to a Big Picture person, they tend to focus on one fact at a time, and this can cause the Big Picture person to feel trapped.

The resolution to this problem is simple once it is identified. When a Big Picture person talks, the Small Picture person should pick one fact that they want to go into detail about when it is their turn to share. The Big Picture person won't mind if you don't remember everything they said. In fact, *they* probably don't remember everything they said. They want to focus on how all the things they said are connected!

Once the Big Picture person is done, the Small Picture person ought to talk about whatever part was mentioned in as much detail as they want. The Big Picture person should focus on how this explanation is connected to the entire picture they presented. When they do, they will find that the Small Picture person is bringing an aspect into high definition, and then the Big Picture person's entire presentation comes into high definition! When the Small Picture person is done talking, the Big Picture person can widen their original presentation, and the exchange between the two people can continue indefinitely.

When two Big Picture people interact, it is easy for one or both of them to ask, "What were we talking about?" after only a few minutes! This is because each person is making the conversation bigger and avoiding details. For two Big Picture people to have a lasting conversation, one of them needs to let the other one go bigger.

When two Small Picture people interact, it is easy for one or both of them to become frustrated. This is because each person makes the conversation smaller, and there's a limit to how specific the two people can get. For example, I know two tiny picture people working on a one-hundred-plus-page grant together, and they had a heated argument over the use of a specific comma! For two Small Picture people to have a lasting conversation, one of the people needs to let the other one go smaller.

When it comes to processing perspective, the key is to remember that Internal Processors will speak once they have made a decision, which makes it look like they are stubborn. External Processors speak to come to a decision. Internal Processors need to avoid holding the External Processor to their words until they have stated they are done processing.

EXAMPLES

Greg is a Big Picture, External Processing, Exhorter-Compassion, and he is married to Mary, a Big Picture, External Processing Server-Giver. This couple immediately hit it off when they were dating and got married very quickly.

It didn't take long to realize Mary is bigger picture than Greg, so Greg needed to go small picture for someone to be aware of the details. Everyone saw them as the life of the party because they were both very expressive and spent a lot of time in groups.

Even though there isn't a lot of tension between the two, they never seemed to experience a joyful, freeing connection with each other. However, they always seemed to be able to do it in groups because of the other individuals present. Worse, Mary wasn't happy. However, being Server-Giver, she was never going to share this until things got so bad and the relationship ended in a bitter and dramatic divorce.

Russell is a Small Picture, Internal Processing Teacher-Perceiver, and he is married to Kate, a Small Picture, Internal Processing Perceiver-Teacher. The couple felt immediately comfortable with each other and got married very quickly. They were very content to keep to themselves and avoid a life of drama. However, something was just a little off, and they couldn't put their finger on it. It turns out that although their tension was only a 1, their ability to get a freeing feeling from connection was also a 1, which means they never felt like they could get relief from the tension even though it wouldn't be very strong. It took years for this marriage to come to an end, and when it did, it was amicable.

Adam is a Big Picture, External Processing Exhorter-Perceiver, and he is married to Lisa, a Small Picture, Internal Processing Giver-Server. Lisa was initially attracted to Adam's enthusiasm for her suggestions and her ability to be a calming force in his life. Over time she has been energized by how much Adam needs her attention to detail, clear-headedness, and ability to bond with him over perceiving while supporting his dreams of success.

> **THIS DEPTH OF CONNECTION AND COMMUNICATION CAN BE INCREDIBLY HEALING AND EXHILARATING.**

Eric is a Small Picture, Internal Processing Server-Server, and he is married to Ellen, a Big Picture, External Processing Exhorter-Compassion. Eric has made Ellen's life fulfilling by being a master at recognizing how much tension she can safely handle and adjusting accordingly. When she is having tough times, he moves to Exhorter-Compassion. When she's feeling confident, he will move to Giver-Compassion or Compassion-Compassion. When she wants to experience tension, he moves to Perceiver-Compassion.

Ralph is a Tiny Picture, very Internal Processing Compassion-Server, and he is married to Mariam, an extremely Big Picture, completely External Processing Server-Server. This couple seems to be completely opposite, and it is the only way either of them will be happy. Anyone who is less internal than Ralph will be interrupting Mariam because she seems unable to think without speaking. This means she states everything she's thinking, even things that could hurt Ralph's feelings. However, Ralph is Compassion-Server and wants to bear this pain. Also, anyone less detailed than Ralph would be unable to help Mariam keep her life together. The marriage shows how the extent of a person's picture perspective is most effectively matched by someone who has the same extent in the opposite direction: slightly big with slightly small, etc. Mariam can be completely herself because of Ralph, who can be completely himself and enjoy life because of Mariam.

Joe is a Big Picture, External Processing Administrator-Perceiver, and he is married to Lilly, a Small Picture, Internal Processing Perceiver-Perceiver. They have a significant amount of tension because they have opposite perspectives and their WHYs are 5 units apart. Joe wants people to be administrated for the future, and Lilly wants to make them aware of the past. Those are very different objectives. But how they want to help people is through perceiving. So, this significant amount of tension results in a massive release (connection) when they come together and connect at Perceiver.

So as you can see, a key component to finding, nourishing, and increasing healthy relationships is understanding your uniqueness, as well as the uniqueness of the person you are (or desire to be) in a relationship with. When you both know and accept your uniqueness, communicating it will result in feeling known and understood in a way you never have before. This depth of connection and communication can be incredibly healing and exhilarating.

But as I've also shown in the examples, with relationships in which people don't know or accept each others' uniquenesses or are unwilling or unable to adjust to that uniqueness, the results can be tragic. In the next chapter, we will learn how to identify and heal unhealthy relationships and trauma.

CHAPTER 12

TRAUMA, DYSFUNCTION, AND UNHEALTHY RELATIONSHIPS

A RECENT tool gaining popularity in predicting mental health disorders and dysfunction is ACE (Adverse Childhood Experiences). Studies have shown a correlation between specific experiences that occur before eighteen years old and a heightened risk for destructive tendencies, like suicide, alcohol abuse, and domestic violence.

The ACE test consists of ten questions that provide a score from 0 to 10. Higher scores have been correlated to higher statistics in everything from mental disorder diagnoses to liver disease.

I'll include the ten questions below. Take a moment to determine your ACE score. You get one point for each question you answer with a "yes."

1. Did a parent or other adult in the household often or very often swear at you, insult you, put you down, or humiliate you, or act in a way that made you afraid that you might be physically hurt?
2. Did a parent or other adult in the household often or very often push, grab, slap, or throw something at you, or ever hit you so hard that you had marks or were injured?
3. Did an adult or person at least 5 years older than you ever touch or fondle you or have you touch their body in a sexual way, or attempt or actually have oral, anal, or vaginal intercourse with you?
4. Did you often or very often feel that no one in your family loved you or thought you were important or special, or your family didn't look out for each other, feel close to each other, or support each other?
5. Did you often or very often feel that you didn't have enough to eat, had to wear dirty clothes, and had no one to protect you, or your parents were too drunk or high to take care of you or take you to the doctor if you needed it?
6. Were your parents ever separated or divorced?
7. Was your mother or stepmother often or very often pushed, grabbed, slapped, or had something thrown at her, or sometimes, often, or very often kicked, bitten, hit with a fist, or hit with something hard, or ever repeatedly hit over at least a few minutes or threatened with a gun or knife?
8. Did you live with anyone who was a problem drinker or alcoholic, or who used street drugs?
9. Was a household member depressed or mentally ill, or did a household member attempt suicide?
10. Did a household member go to prison?

Below are some statistics for various problems that occur later in life, correlated with a higher ACE score.

Reported Alcoholic:	Perpetrating domestic violence:
0: 3%	0: 3%
1: 6%	1: 4%
2: 10%	2: 5%
3: 11%	3: 7%
4+: 16%	4+: 11%
Depression:	Suicide Attempts:
0: 13%	0: 1%
1: 21%	1: 3%
2: 30%	2: 5%
3: 35%	3: 10%
4+: 45%	4+: 19%

The ACE score seems to be a relatively good statistical predictor of future mental, social, and drug abuse problems. Schools have adopted this sort of statistical analysis for determining informed care for children with emotional and behavioral disorders, meaning they take into account the past trauma when attempting to understand behaviors and treat the children.

ACE is a good statistical tool but doesn't cover all the bases. Not everyone who experiences a score of four or more on an ACE test is guaranteed to struggle later in life. Not everyone who scores a 0 is guaranteed to not struggle later in life.

Experts have recently realized the main challenge with this tool is that it doesn't account for uniqueness! We have updated the tool so that it not only increased its accuracy, but it helps anticipate potential issues so they could be addressed earlier or potentially avoided completely!

Updated model: Trauma x Intangible Driver x Intangible Driver of role-model adult

The role of trauma is still essential to understand. However, even experts are realizing there are traumatic experiences that aren't covered by the ACE test. Everyone experiences trauma. But another critical variable is to understand the Intangible Driver of the person being assessed.

Over the last decade, we have seen that the more future-focused the individual's ID, the more likely the trauma will appear not to affect them. For example, one client was a successful woman who had four sisters. All five of these women had an ACE score well over 6. The successful woman we worked with is Future-Future (a combination of Exhorter, Administrator, or Server). She had a sister who is also Future-Future who seemed to be doing well. Her Past-Future sister had some issues, while her two Past-Past sisters weren't doing quite as well. One was on medication while the other had been committed to a mental health facility.

We have approximately an 85% accuracy rate with the initial result from the Intangible Driver quiz. It is not 100% because approximately 15% of people answer in line with their role-model adult. The final variable is the Intangible Driver of the role-model adult.

While this tends to be fathers for males and mothers for females, the role-model adult is the person their unconscious saw as the adult they were most influenced by during their formative years. During these crucial years, the unconscious learns from the child's conscious and subconscious choices the behaviors it believes it is supposed to demonstrate when it emulates its role-model adult.

The Intangible Driver of the role-model adult can have a healthy or unhealthy impact on the person. For example, the person could have a high ACE score, be Past-Past in their Intangible Driver, yet their role-model adult's influence as a Compassion-Server could mute out the effects seen by other people who had similar circumstances. On the other hand, a person with a low to no ACE score and non-Past-Past Intangible Driver could have seemingly overwhelming issues due to their role-model adult being Teacher-Perceiver.

WE HAVE SEEN THAT THE MORE FUTURE-FOCUSED THE INDIVIDUAL'S ID, THE MORE LIKELY THE TRAUMA WILL APPEAR NOT TO AFFECT THEM.

Notice, it is never healthy for the child to take on the Intangible Driver of the role-model adult. Even if the child has a "difficult" ID (Perceiver-Exhorter), it is even more unhealthy in the long term for the child to try to become the role-model adult, even if the role model has a "nice" ID (Compassion-Server).

We see this information sheds light on the real influence of the role-model adult. This means understanding how to adjust this influence either as a role-model adult or a counselor can have a considerable impact. Let's look at some examples.

My friend Rob is an Exhorter-Server whose father is a Perceiver-Perceiver. Growing up, Rob always wanted to chase the future. He liked to go to skateparks and ride BMX bikes and got into trouble at school by being very outspoken. Being an Exhorter, he had big emotions, and he wore his emotions on his sleeve. He paired that with a strong sense of justice, which would get him into arguments with teachers and principals.

Rob's dad responded to this behavior at first by trying to clamp down more limitations and trying to ground him, but this caused

Rob to push harder to have more freedom. His dad kept trying to perceive, pushing Rob to see and accept reality, that things weren't always going to feel fair.

When Rob recounts his relationship with his dad years later, he remarks that it seemed like his dad changed overnight. One day instead of responding with yelling and stricter rules, his dad let up. Rob realized that his dad started focusing on feeling what Rob was feeling instead of trying to get Rob to accept reality.

When Rob looked back at this time in his life, he realized it didn't make sense. When he asked his dad what happened, why his dad suddenly changed his behavior, his dad said, "I realized that if something didn't change, our relationship could be destroyed. I didn't want that, and I didn't think you would be the one to change. So I adjusted."

Now, Rob and his dad have a great relationship, and it's because his dad adjusted to Rob's uniqueness instead of pushing harder to get Rob to adjust to his and see reality.

The second example is when a role model is not present during development years. Whether that means the role model abandons the child, is mentally checked out, or is not present due to work, it doesn't matter. The lack of a role model being present acts in the same way as a misaligned Intangible Driver.

When Andrew, a Server-Server, was young, his relationship with his dad was great. There was empathy, connection, and safety. When Andrew reached his teenage years, his father started drinking heavily. While there was never physical abuse, his father checked out mentally, resulting in Andrew feeling like he'd suddenly lost his role model, and he didn't find a new role model to replace him. Without someone to look up to for how he should be growing, Andrew began to spiral downwards, struggling with depression, bipolar disorder, and even attempting suicide.

Andrew's ACE score is only 2, but the lack of a role model made even a low score cause significant damage in his life. It wasn't until Andrew learned his Intangible Driver and learned how to be himself that he could grow past his former struggles and repair his damage with his dad.

Applying Intangible Drivers is also the key to resolving the problems that arise due to a high ACE score. It isn't about whether or not a child has an adverse experience. It matters how that experience is handled.

> **IT ISN'T ABOUT WHETHER OR NOT A CHILD HAS AN ADVERSE EXPERIENCE. IT MATTERS HOW THAT EXPERIENCE IS HANDLED.**

I've worked closely with women who have been assaulted. When the first person they told had compassion and listened well, even though this is a profoundly terrifying trauma, it didn't have as deep and long-lasting effects as when the first person they told showed little compassion and didn't listen well.

Many people who have been abused can repair the damage and live their lives without experiencing significant emotional trauma when the first person they told heard it well. This is why it is imperative that first responders, law enforcement, and medical personnel all be trained in how to hear a traumatic story well. We never know who will be the first to hear it.

On the other hand, I've known women who were assaulted, and the first person they told handled it terribly. Many women have shared that when the first person they told was their mother, the mother responded by screaming and crying because she felt she had failed as a mother. The abused women would have to comfort their mothers, even though *she* was the one who had the traumatic experience!

So, instead of being able to deal with her trauma, her first experience sharing it would make it worse. Instead of getting help, she would now feel like sharing her trauma would cause more pain to others. Instead of processing and repairing her trauma, it could end up defining her.

It isn't just anyone who can have this effect on us. It's our role models. Are you beginning to see the connection between these adverse experiences and how they are handled?

The statistical analysis of adverse childhood experiences is a fantastic tool to indicate what kinds of problems students and children might run into later in life, but it does have gaps. By applying Intangible Drivers, we can fill in these gaps and explain why outcomes vary. We can even anticipate challenging circumstances and address them proactively.

Let's conclude this book by looking at how Intangible Drivers give the template for repairing trauma.

CHAPTER 13

GENERATIVITY

WHEN TED abuses Kyle, how many victims are there?

Most people think the obvious answer is "one" - the person who was abused. However, the person doing the abuse was also a victim. Otherwise, why is Ted abusing Kyle?

More to the point, how do you think we ought to address this issue? There are four options.

First, we can ignore it in hopes that it goes away. We know it will only result in the abuse continuing.

Second, we can punish Ted. How does that help Kyle? Yes, it puts an end to the immediate abuse, but does this mean Kyle is healed? Are we sure this isn't the same approach used towards Ted when his dad abused him? Worse, how does this approach help Ted? Is it any wonder abuse continues to run rampant despite hundreds of years using this approach?

Third, we can give counseling to Ted and Kyle. However, both people will still be wary of the other person and become worn out, having to continually effort or force their way through a series of steps meant to repair the abuse.

Now we see why the second option looks better because at least Kyle can rest knowing it is less likely Ted will abuse him again. However, both people will spend the rest of their lives living with the abuse and trying not to think about it simultaneously.

It is no wonder why most counselors' goal is sustainability. They try to help the victims of abuse not harm themselves and consider it a win when they don't. The implication is that both people will never achieve their hopes and dreams, or become something more, by surviving at this level.

There is a fourth option, and it is Generativity. It is the option where both people end up better *because* of the abuse! Each individual can grow in happiness and profitability over time by becoming more of who they were made to be, and they are willing to talk about the abuse.

The template for this process is the Intangible Drivers. Let's think about it this way. When you hurt someone, what are you supposed to do?

Let's say that you were frustrated, and you yelled at a friend and realized you'd hurt their feelings. What's your next course of action? Most people would apologize. What is an apology?

You tell the other person you feel bad that you hurt their feelings. Does that make everything better? What if it was something worse? Apologize with more feeling?

An apology addresses the symptom of the problem, which is our feelings. An apology boils down to just sharing that someone feels bad.

If I broke your windshield, an apology wouldn't pay for the damages, and it certainly wouldn't make the windshield better than it was before. But this is possible with Generativity. Being Generative doesn't just fix the issue. It makes it better!

ADMISSION

The first step to Generativity is to admit what you did wrong! Notice, an apology doesn't have to admit what someone did. In fact, the word "apology" comes from the Greek word meaning "a speech in one's defense"! An apology is wholly focused on the wrongdoer avoiding admission and focusing on defending themselves!

The first part of the admission begins with Perceiver. That is, it starts by stating what was wrong. "I was wrong to...."

Notice, admitting it was wrong of you to yell at your friend is a good start. However, your friend could think, "How do I know you won't do it again? You don't even know why you did it."

Then we move to Teacher, explaining why it was done. "I did it because...."

While this is good, your friend could think, "Okay, so you know why it happened, but maybe you just like yelling at me and want to do it again."

Finally, you state that you don't want to do it again, which is Compassion because you're sharing how you feel. Obviously, if you don't actually feel that way, you aren't ready to step into this process. That's why this step is the Compassion step. We actually need to *feel* it.

This three-step process is a Full Admission. The benefit of this process is that it helps the other person to feel safe. When I hurt others, it causes a change in their brain. That pain causes them to rethink their relationship with me and causes them to feel unsafe.

If I were to wrong someone and go through this full admission process, it reestablishes that safety. When I say I'm wrong, the person feels like I see what they see. When I give my reason, it provides a new perspective and shows them that my *intention* was not to hurt them. This helps because we often lump the behavior and intention of others and feel like people *meant* to do the things they did, even when they didn't, such as a bully who is trying to be funny but tells a hurtful joke without realizing it.

If we give our reason without stating that we're wrong, it will make the situation worse because the person we wronged will feel like we're telling them why we're right. They'll feel more confident that we will hurt them again and feel less safe!

Finally, the person could feel like we might still do it again. After all, we all do things that we know are wrong. Stating that we don't *want* to do it again allows people to feel like we actually want to change.

While this is good, the person still has a negative emotion attached to the event of you yelling at them. Now it's time to step into the next part of the process, which is Repair.

REPAIR

Restoration means that something has been returned to its original state. Repair means it is being fixed to a greater state than the original.

Repairing involves Giver and Server. We are trying to give to the person to make up for what we did wrong. "I will do this...," which is Giver. "Is there something else that I can do to make it up to you?" which is Server.

The goal is to make up for it in a fashion that the person now feels good about the abuse. For example, how would you feel if I slapped you across the face? Would you want to tell others about it? Now, what if I gave you a million dollars? How would you feel about being slapped across the face? Would you want to tell others about it?

Notice, the one thing that people want more than anything is something that is in line with their Intangible Driver. This is another reason why Repair seems to be difficult. We think the method ought to be the same for everyone regardless of their uniqueness. As if we all value things the same. However, Repairing according to a person's uniqueness is healing.

Do you see how this is different from an apology? By the time we make it to Server, assuming we've done it well, we've re-established a safe feeling and made up for what we've done to the point the emotion attached to the incident is positive. One could even argue that by sharing our intention, we've helped the person to have a less negative emotion to that type of behavior in the future. On top of that, the person might have built up some trust that if we do something wrong, we're going to make up for it. That'll help them feel safe in the future if something does go wrong, and it breeds patience.

This is already generative, and we haven't even finished. We've established a way to take a negative experience and use it to build trust and patience.

MORE

From here, we can look at the Administrator and Exhorter steps. The Administrator step looks at the other people who were affected by what we did wrong. For example, when you yelled at your friend, you probably felt unsettled by it. To defend yourself, you may have told others how your friend did something that made you yell at him. You have admitted your wrong to everyone except your friend, and now people think less of your friend.

The Administrator step would now go to all these people you talked to so you could Exhort them about how good your friend actually is! Think about it this way. The surrounding people may not have had an impression of your friend. After you defend yourself, they will think less of your friend. Once you Exhort them as to how your friend handled themselves well and it was you who was wrong, these people will think more highly of your friend than they did initially.

There is one more way people will form a higher opinion, and it is hidden. What do you think of others who admit it when they are wrong? Don't you think more highly of them? What do you think others will think of you when you admit you are wrong?

The last four steps of the Generative process is Full Repair. Everyone ends up with more!

Margaret's two children, an Exhorter and a Teacher, often make this mistake. The Teacher thinks the Exhorter intends to cause him pain when the Exhorter is trying to help him have fun. The Teacher may complain, "No, he's trying to make everyone else miserable! Because he's miserable!" and then he tries to get revenge.

I'm going to be clear: there is a *gap* between our intentions and our behaviors. We feel like *our* intentions automatically show through, and everyone should see them, but we turn around and feel like *other* people's intentions line up with their behavior. It is natural, it is intuitive, but it is untrue. When we practice full admission and full repair, we close the gap between our behavior and our intentions. It helps us get more connected with other people as an effect of something going wrong. If we have a generative moment, like in full admission and full repair, we actually feel *good* that a bad thing happened.

The profitability of any community, including a family, a group of friends, or a work environment, is directly related to how much we share, minus how much we abuse (which will happen in any community), plus how much we repair.

If we repair enough, we can completely offset the abuse. But we can never share enough to overcome the abuse that happens over time. In other words, we can never be sustainable in a community. We will either be generative and keep building up the community over time into a better and better state, or we'll be destructive in the long-term, breaking it down further and further over time.

The key to generative communities is embracing uniqueness and allowing each person's uniqueness to come through to help the community become something more. It is accomplished by each person growing in who they are and allowing others to focus *more* on being themselves.

I'll leave you with a few questions that we ask middle schoolers to prepare them for their teenage years. We want to help them have fun and excitement during this time in their life.

What kind of community do you want to have around you?

Are your friends the same uniqueness as you, or are they different?

Are you able to handle the tension of interacting with someone different from you to get more energy from being yourself?

You now have all the tools to begin building a generative community, or as I like to say, "your band." You now have a choice. You can intentionally choose to live your life ignoring the truth of who you and others are. You can keep sticking band aids over your trauma and wasting enormous amounts of time and energy on "fixing" problems that will continue to be problems and ultimately create more problems. Or, you can take a step back, put this powerful information into action in your life, and watch as you become a stronger, more confident, happier you. Now that you have unlocked your instrument, it's time to make music with others so that you can play the amazing song that your life was meant to be!

www.ingramcontent.com/pod-product-compliance
Lightning Source LLC
Chambersburg PA
CBHW071832230426
43672CB00013B/2820